# *IRISH SAGAS*
## *AND*
# *FOLK TALES*

*Retold by*

EILEEN O'FAOLAIN

*Illustrated by*

JOAN
KIDDELL-MONROE

Avenel Books
New York

# Acknowledgments

Acknowledgment is made to Messrs. George G. Harrap & Co., Ltd., for permission to quote *Beside the Fire* and *May Day* from *The High Deeds of Finn* by T. W. Rolleston; and to Mr. Donn S. Piatt for permission to quote *Cuchullin's Lament for Ferdia* from George Sigerson's *Bards of the Gael and Gall*; and to Mrs. W. B. Yeats and Messrs. Macmillan & Co., Ltd., for permission to quote the eight lines on page 175.



This 1982 edition is published by Avenel Books, distributed by Crown Publishers, Inc. by arrangement with Eileen O'Faolain

Manufactured in the United States of America

**Library of Congress Cataloging in Publication Data**

O'Faolain, Eileen.
Irish sagas and folk tales.

Summary: Twenty-one stories from Ireland, including heroic sagas, ancestral tales of men and gods, stories about the Fianna, a band of warrior-athletes, and tales of fairies and leprechauns.
1. Tales—Ireland. [1. Folklore—Ireland] I. Kiddell-Monroe, Joan, ill.
II. Title.
PZ8.1.033Ir 1982 398.2'09415 82-8859
AACR2

ISBN: 0-517-391007

h g f e d c b

# CONTENTS

## From the Dawn of Time



## In the Time of Cuchullin



## In the Time of Finn and the Fianna

## *Tales for the Chimney-Corner*

# *FROM THE DAWN OF TIME*

## *The Three Most Famous Tales*

Three sorrows of story-telling fill me with pity,
the telling of them grates on the ear;
the woe of the Children of Turenn—
sorrowful to hear.

And the Children of Lir, bird-shaped;
a curse on the mouth that told their doom:
Conn, Fiacra, Finola, and Aed—
the second gloom.

And the Children of Usnach, shield of men,
who fell by force and cunning craft—
Naisi, and Ainle, and Ardan . . .
There cracks the heart.

*From the Irish*

# I

# THE QUEST OF THE CHILDREN OF TURENN

## (*The first sorrow of story-telling*)

A COUPLE of thousand years ago there lived in Ireland a people who were gods and the children of gods. They were of radiant beauty and godlike bearing, and they loved above all things poetry, music and beauty of form in man and woman. These beautiful people were descended from the goddess Dana, and so were called the De Danaans, or the People of Dana.

It happened that at this time Ireland was frequently raided by savage bands of sea-robbers, called the Fomorians, who swept down from their land in the northern mists and drove away cattle and pillaged the country. They also put heavy taxes on the People of Dana. Each year a tax had to be paid on every quern stone, used for grinding the wheat into flour, and on every kneading-trough, for mixing the dough, and on the baking-flags for baking it. In addition to these there was a poll tax amounting to one ounce of gold on each man, and anyone neglecting to pay this tribute had the nose cut from his face without mercy.

Balor of the Evil Eye was King of the Fomorians, and

he was held in the greatest dread by the people of Ireland. His one eye, which was all he had, had but to glance at an enemy for him to drop dead as if struck by a thunderbolt. But as Balor grew old, the great, flabby eyelid drooped over the deadly eye, and it had to be hoisted up by pulleys and ropes, and the eye directed by his men on the one he wished to destroy. In addition to this there was no weapon made which could kill Balor, so the people of Ireland, under their King Nuada of the Silver Hand, decided to pay their taxes and give tribute, instead of trying to resist such a powerful enemy. But every day they grew impatient of the tyranny of their oppressors, and longed for a brave leader who would lead them to victory against the invaders.

Just at this time a young warrior called Lugh of the Long Arm appeared in Ireland. Though really one of the People of Dana, he had been reared by the Faery, and when he left their land, on coming to manhood, he brought with him valuable magical gifts. He had ' Wave-Sweeper ', the boat of Manannan Mac Lir, the sea-god. This knew its owner's mind and could go over the land as readily as it could go on the water, and it was said to be as quick as the naked March wind. He also had a powerful sword called ' The Answerer ', and that could cut its way through iron of any thickness. So just when all hope of throwing out the cruel Fomorians seemed dead, a whisper went around the country of the sudden appearance of a beautiful young man, whose face shone like the setting sun, and who walked the earth like a god. Lugh's fame spread, and soon nothing else was talked of up and down the country but the valour of his deeds and the beauty of his person, and so famous did he become that now the rainbow was called the sling of Lugh, and the Milky Way—that path of starry brightness that crosses the heavens on a frosty night—was christened the chain of Lugh.

Now, when Lugh's name was on every lip it happened that the yearly tribute, or payment of taxes, to the Fomorians fell due. As was usual, King Nuada and his nobles waited on the Hill of Usnach near Tara, the residence of the High Kings, for the tax-gatherers from Balor to arrive to get their money. As they sat there the royal company saw a strange cavalcade riding towards them across the plain, and at their head was a young warrior riding a white horse. As he drew nearer they noticed that a light like the sun shone from his face and from the precious stones which studded the helmet on his head. As the cavalcade reined in their horses, King Nuada and his nobles bade them welcome and invited them to take a seat among them.

But soon their talk was interrupted by the arrival, from the other side of the hill, of a band of swarthy, evil-looking fellows who spoke disdainfully to the King. These were the Fomorian tax-gatherers, and there were nine times nine of them. King Nuada and his nobles rose to show the tax-gatherers their respect, and when the bright-faced warrior, who had come on the white horse, saw them standing for this surly-looking, mean group, he inquired of the King:

'Why do you rise for this ill-visaged, low-bred band, when you did not rise for me, Lugh of the Long Arm?'

Then, finding out that the ugly group for whom the King stood were the tax-gatherers of Balor, Lugh reproached him, and straightway fell upon the tax-gatherers, and killed all but a few, whom he sent back to Balor with insolent messages and without their taxes.

Balor then prepared his armies and his ships to make dreadful war on the people of Erin, and, calling together his captains, he gave them their orders:

'Give battle to Lugh of the Long Arm, and cut off his head, and tie that island that is called Erin to the stern of your ships and, letting the dense, verging waters close over it, tow it northwards to the cold, dark regions where none of the people of Dana will ever find it again.'

In the meantime news was brought to King Nuada that the Fomorians had landed in the west. Lugh incited the King to resist them and drive them out of the land for ever. Then he himself rode westward out of Tara, to gather the people of Faery out of their raths and duns, where they dwelt in the earth-mounds, to help him in the coming war. On his way he met his own father Kian with his two brothers, Cu and Ceithin. They offered to help him to muster the warriors of Faery, so Cu and Ceithin went to the south, while Lugh's father, Kian, took the road to the north.

Crossing the plain of Muirthemne, Kian saw three warriors in full battle array coming towards him. As they came closer he saw that they were the three Sons of Turenn, with whom his family had an old feud. Kian knew that if they recognized him he could not avoid a contest with them, and as he was single-handed against three, he made up his mind to retreat.

Looking around he saw a herd of swine grazing near him, so, striking himself with a druidic wand, he changed himself into a pig and began to root the ground with the rest.

Brian, the eldest of the Sons of Turenn, asked his brothers if they knew what had happened to the warrior who, but a little while ago, had been riding towards them.

'We do not know,' they replied.

'It is a shame for you not to keep your eyes open in times like these,' said Brian, and then he told them that the warrior had turned himself into a pig and was hiding himself among the herd.

'That puts us into a dilemma,' said the brothers, 'for we cannot tell which is the enchanted pig, and even if we kill them all, the one we want may escape us in the end.'

'Badly have you learned your lesson in the City of Learning,' said Brian, 'to say you cannot tell a druidical pig from a natural one,' and he struck them with a wand and turned his brothers into two swift hounds, which ran after the enchanted pig at once, and began to yelp madly at him.

The pig made for a little wood, with the hounds after him, but just as he reached it Brian, casting his spear after him, drove it clean through his body.

The wounded pig then spoke in a human voice and asked for quarter, and Brian refused.

Then the pig asked to be allowed to resume his human shape before being killed, and this Brian granted.

Then, having taken his own shape, Kian said:

'Now I ask for quarter as a man, for if you kill me now you will pay the blood fine on a man, and not on a pig. And I warn you that the blood fine that you will pay on me will be heavier than was ever paid before on any living person. And whatever arms you may use to kill me will cry out and tell of your crime to my son, Lugh of the Long Arm.'

'It is not with weapons we will kill you, but with the stones of the road only,' said Brian.

And so the Sons of Turenn started, and they cast stones at Kian, and they did not stop till he fell in one broken heap on the ground and his body was a litter of wounds. Then they buried him his own depth in the ground, and went off to join in the war against the Fomorians.

In that battle Lugh and his people, helped by the warriors from Faeryland, routed the invaders and sent them back to their land in the northern mists. Then Lugh called his kinsmen to him and asked for tidings of his father, Kian. They said they had not seen him since the eve of the battle when he went north to muster the Faery host.

'I know he is not living,' said Lugh, 'and I pledge my word not to touch food or drink till I find out how he came by his death.'

Then he went back to the last place he had seen his father, and after that on to the Plain of Muirthemne, where Kian had met the Sons of Turenn. Here the stones of the ground cried out to Lugh and told him of the killing of his father by the Sons of Turenn.

Lugh stopped and ordered his men to dig up the grave, that he might see in what manner his father had been done to death.

The body was raised out of the earth, and they looked at it and saw that it was one litter of wounds.

Lugh bent down and kissed his father three times, and then, jumping to his feet, said to his men:

'This death has so grieved me that I can neither see with my eyes, nor hear with my ears, nor is there a living pulse-beat left in my heart with grief for my father. It was the Sons of Turenn did this thing, and sorrow and anguish will fall on them because of it and on their children after them.'

Then he ordered the body to be put back in the earth, and he and his followers made their way to Tara, where the High King Nuada was celebrating the victory against the Fomorians.

When Lugh reached Tara he was conducted to an honourable place at the King's right hand. As he sat there in the assembly he looked around at the warriors and nobles present, and his eye fell on the three Sons of Turenn. The minute he did Lugh stood up and asked that the Chain of Silence be shaken, as he wished to speak to all present, and this is what he said:

'O King and warriors of Ireland, I ask you to tell me what vengeance would each of you take on him who had murdered your father?'

Each one present looked at the other and all were astonished. Then the King spoke and asked if it was Lugh's own father who had been killed.

'It is indeed my own father who has been murdered,' said Lugh, 'and I see here in this house the men who killed him, and they know themselves how they killed him better than I can tell them.'

King Nuada was the first to give his verdict, and this is what he said:

'It is not on the one day I would kill the man who had made an end of my father, but I would cut off a limb day by day, till he would come to his death.'

All the chief men and warriors agreed with this, and the Sons of Turenn no less than the rest.

Then Lugh said that he would not demand the life of those who had killed Kian, since they were of the People of Dana, his own people; but instead he would ask them to pay a fine, and that they should make no attempt to leave the Royal Assembly until they had pledged themselves to pay it.

Then the Sons of Turenn stood up and asked Lugh what his fine was to be, for now they saw that Lugh knew of their guilt.

'This,' said Lugh, 'is the fine I am asking:

Three apples,
The skin of a pig,
A spear,
Two horses and a chariot,
Seven pigs,
A puppy dog,
A cooking spit,
Three shouts on a hill.

'And,' said Lugh, 'if it is too much for you, a part will be taken from it, and if you do not think it is too much, then pay it in full.'

'We do not think it is too much,' said Brian, 'nor a hundred times more would not be too much; but we think that there is some treachery in the back of your head, on account of the smallness of your fine.'

'Then I will give you more knowledge of the fine,' said Lugh, and he went on to tell them that the three apples were apples from the Garden of the Hesperides in the Eastern World. 'Those apples,' he said, 'are of the colour of burnished gold, they have the taste of honey, and have the power to cure wounds or any kind of sickness, and they are each the size of the head of a two-months'-old child.

'And the skin of the pig I asked of you belongs to the King of Greece, and it has the power to heal all wounds and all kinds of sickness.

'And the spear I want is the poisoned spear of Pisar, King of Persia. That spear is so active and mad for battle that its blade has to be kept standing always in a cauldron of icy water, for fear it would melt down the city around it with its fiery heat.

'And do you know what two steeds and chariots I would wish to get from you?' he went on.

'We do not know,' said they.

'They are the two steeds of Dobar, the King of Sicily, and they can ride over the sea as if it were land, and there is no chariot equal to that one for strength and beauty of shape.

'And the seven pigs are the pigs of Asal, King of the Golden Pillars,' said Lugh, 'and though they are killed at nightfall, they are found alive again the next day, and they will cure anyone who is sick or in ill-health, and they never grow less with the eating.

'And the dog's whelp I was asking for belongs to the King of Iruad, and all the wild beasts of the world would lie down in fright before her, for she is more resplendent than the sun within its golden wheel.

'The cooking-spit I want is one from the kitchen of the Faery women of Finchory Island, and to find that island is no small task, for it is neither on the sea nor on the land.

'The three shouts on a hill must be given on the Hill of Midcain, in the land of the Northern Mists. Midcain and his three sons are under bonds not to allow anyone to shout on that hill, and as it was with him that my father Kian got his training in arms and war, it is certain that I would forgive you his death sooner than he.

'And such, O Sons of Turenn, is the eric you have to pay for the slaying of Kian, my father.'

The three brothers were struck dumb with despair when they heard what Lugh's fine meant, and they went straight to their father's dun to tell him of the misfortune that had befallen them, and to ask his advice.

'It is a hard fine,' said Turenn, 'but it must be paid, though it bring you to death and destruction.'

Then he advised them to go to Lugh and ask him to lend them 'Wave-sweeper' to take them over the seas on their quest.

They went to Lugh and he gave them the boat, and they

bade farewell to their father, and to their sister Eithne, who sorrowed greatly at their departure. Then they pushed out from the land of Erin and started on their travels.

'We shall go first to the Garden of the Hesperides in the Eastern World and get the apples,' said Brian, and the currach, without any more commands, turned its prow to the east and sailed away over the ridgy waves, and never stopped till it grounded in a little cove under the Garden of the Hesperides where the golden apples grew.

'Now,' said Brian, 'how will we go about getting the apples?'

'Let us march up and fight for them,' said the two younger brothers, 'and if luck be with us we shall get them, or else we shall die fighting, as die we must, before we have paid all Kian's fine.'

'No,' said Brian, 'let us not be foolhardy, but rather let us act with cleverness and skill, so that even if we do die, the bravery of our deed and the wisdom of our actions will live after us. In my opinion,' he went on, 'the best thing for us to do now is to go into the garden in the shape of three swift hawks, and fly around the tree where the apples grow, until the warriors who are guarding it will have shot all their spears and javelins at us. Then we can swoop down, and quickly snatch an apple each, and bear it away in our claws.'

So Brian struck each of them with a druidical wand and changed them into three beautiful, sharp-eyed hawks. Flying around the tree, they evaded the shower of spears that the guards cast at them, and waiting till the last spear and javelin was thrown, they pounced down on the apples, and each hawk bore one away in its claws without suffering even a single scratch.

The news of the raid spread quickly about the city, and the three clever daughters of the King lost no time in turning themselves into three taloned ospreys, and followed them out to sea. As they went they sent shafts of lightning over and under the hawks, scorching their feathers and driving them off their course. But Brian turned himself and his brothers into swans, and darting under the water they escaped from the ospreys.

Then they went back to their boat, where they rested a little, rejoicing that the first of their quests had been successful.

Next they decided to go to Greece and seek the skin of the pig.

'In what guise should we go there?' asked his brothers of Brian.

'We shall go as poets from Erin,' said Brian, 'so that the people of Greece will honour and respect us.'

So the three of them dressed their hair in the poet's way, and when they landed in Greece they went up and knocked at the door of the Royal Palace of King Tuis. When the door-keeper asked them who they were, they answered that they were poets from Ireland, and they had come with a poem for the King.

By the King's order they were invited in and royally feasted. The King's poet sang the songs and poems of Greece for them, and then Brian spoke his poem for the King. He called him 'the oak among kings' and praised him for his hospitality, and then, as a reward for his poem, he asked the King for the skin of the pig that was said to cure all wounds.

The King was pleased with the poem, but he was troubled by the request, and at having to refuse it.

'I would not give that skin to all the poets or men of learning in the wide world,' he declared, 'but I will give you three times the fill of it of red gold, as the price of your poem.'

Brian said he was well satisfied with this reward, but he asked that he should be allowed to see the measuring of the gold into the skin himself.

The King agreed to this, and he went with his two brothers and the King's servants to the treasure-house.

'Now,' said Brian, 'measure out the two shares for my brothers first, and then fill up a good skinful for me, since it was I who made the poem.'

As they were measuring, Brian suddenly snatched the skin from the King's servant and, drawing his sword, prepared to hack his way through the guards. His two brothers joined him and they rushed through the palace, cutting down

all who stood in their way. Just as they reached the door, King Tuis himself rushed on Brian and engaged him in single combat. Many and deadly were the blows they exchanged, until at last Brian drove his sword through the King's body, and so King Tuis of Greece fell by the hand of Brian, Son of Turenn. When they got to the shore they jumped into their boat and made out to sea, and they rested for a while and cured their wounds by laying on them the skin of the magic pig. Then, as the blue-watered land of

Greece faded behind them, they decided to go to Persia and seek the spear of King Pisar.

It was agreed that they would go to King Pisar's Court in the guise of poets once again. So, putting the tie of poets on their hair, they appeared at the door of the palace. As in Greece, they were brought in and treated with honour and respect as poets from the distant land of Erin. Then Brian chanted a poem in praise of King Pisar and of his magic spear.

'That is a good poem,' said the King, 'but I cannot understand why you bring my spear into it, oh man of Poetry from Erin.'

Brian said that he would like to have the spear as a reward for his poem.

The King grew very angry at hearing this, and said:

'It is the greatest possible reward that you are not put to death instantly for making such a request.'

No sooner had Brian heard the King's refusal than he threw one of the three golden apples from the Garden of the Hesperides at his head and dashed out his brains. Before the King's warriors could recover from their surprise, Brian and his brothers made for the courtyard, where they had seen the spear steeping in a cauldron of ice-water to keep it from scorching the people and burning down the city. They seized the spear, and fought their way down to the boat, and many and grievous were the wounds they gave and received before they reached 'Wave-sweeper' and pushed out to sea once more.

'Now,' said Brian, 'let us go to Sicily and ask King Dobar for the two steeds and the chariot that Lugh of the Long Arm demands of us. Let us tell Dobar that we are Irish soldiers wishing to hire ourselves out to the kings of the world. Then, when we take service with him, we shall see where he keeps the two magic horses and the chariot, and how we can come at them.'

As they hoped, King Dobar was pleased to hire the three brothers, and they entered into his service. But they were at his Court for a month and two weeks, and never in all that time did they catch as much as a glimpse of the steeds or the chariot. So Brian began to lose patience, and he said to his brothers:

'It is little use for us to wait here any longer, for we know as much of the horses and chariot that we came to get as we did on the first day of our hiring.'

'What shall we do, then?' they asked him.

'Gather together your belongings,' said Brian, 'and gird on your arms and your travelling array. Then let us go to the King, and let us tell him that we will leave his service unless he shows us his steeds and his chariot that are famous throughout the Western World.'

And they did as Brian said, and they went to the King dressed as if for a journey, and the King, wishing to keep them in his service, sent for his steeds and had them yoked to the chariot. Then he had them driven around the show-ground, so that Brian and his brothers could see them, and they saw that the steeds could go on the water as if it were dry land, and they were as quick as the thin wind of March.

Brian was watching the steeds carefully, and, as they were passing him the second time he made a sudden spring, and, leaping into the chariot, seized the reins, and dashed the charioteer from his seat. His two brothers were quickly by his side and, before the King and his nobles knew what was happening, the Sons of Turenn had driven away his steeds and chariot, and so ended their fourth quest.

By this time, having come through so many trials safely, the three brothers began to feel that perhaps they would succeed in fulfilling Lugh's eric. So their spirits rose, and they journeyed happily on to the Land of the Golden Pillars to get the seven magic pigs from King Asal.

As their boat touched the shore, Asal, to their surprise, came down to the brink of the water to meet them. He told them that the fame of their deeds had spread throughout the world, and he asked them if it were true that they had plundered the treasures of the kings of the world for the payment of a mighty blood fine.

Then Brian told him the story of the eric that Lugh had

put on them, and of the trials and hardships they had already suffered in trying to pay it.

'And now,' said King Asal, 'why have you come to my country?'

'We have come,' said Brian, 'for your seven magic pigs, for they too are part of that eric.'

When the King heard this he took counsel with his people, and they decided to give up the pigs peacefully to the Sons of Turenn, partly to show admiration for their valiant deeds and partly because they knew that the Sons of Turenn would get them, as they got the other treasures in the lands they had already visited.

Brian and his brothers then swore fealty to King Asal, and pledged themselves to stand by his side and fight to the death for him in whatever quarrel he might find himself. Then King Asal took them to his palace for the night, and they were given every kind of food and drink and soft beds to lie on.

When they arose in the morning Asal asked them what country they intended to visit next.

'We are going to Iruad,' said they, 'for a puppy hound that the King has.'

'Grant me one request,' said Asal, 'and that is to allow me to go with you to Iruad, for a daughter of mine is married to the king, and I want to persuade him to give that puppy to you without striking a blow.'

So the King's boat was got ready, and the Sons of Turenn arranged their treasures in 'Wave-sweeper', and they set out together for the land of Iruad.

When they reached it they found all the coves and the harbours guarded against them, and they were forbidden to land. Asal, however, went to his son-in-law, told him the whole story of the Sons of Turenn, and how they had to fight the kings and mighty warriors of the world to get their treasures for Lugh of the Long Arm in payment of the blood fine he put on his father. He advised him to give them the puppy hound in a peaceful way, and reminded him that many of the kings of the world had already fallen by their swords.

But the King of Iruad would take no such advice.

'There are no champions born,' said he, 'that the gods have so favoured that they could get my puppy hound either by force or by goodwill.'

When the Sons of Turenn heard this they quickly seized their weapons and rushed upon the King and his guards. Fierce and bloody was the conflict that was waged around the brothers, and they were separated many times. At last Brian came on the King in the thick of the fight, and he engaged him in single combat, and succeeded in overpowering him. Then he bore him through the centre of the fighting throng to where Asal was at the side, outside the press of battle.

'There is your son-in-law for you,' said he to King Asal, 'and I swear by my arms of valour it would have been easier for me to kill him three times over than to bring him here to you.'

So peace was made between them, and the King of Iruad gladly gave them his hound in admiration of their valiant fight. And it was in the friendliest spirit that they bade farewell to the two kings and set out to sea once more.

Meanwhile, back in Erin, Lugh had discovered, by means of sorcery, that the Sons of Turenn had obtained all the magical treasures that he needed in the coming battle against the Fomorians, for the last battle of that war had not so far been fought. He knew that their eric was not yet complete, for they had not got the cooking-spit nor had they given the three shouts on the Hill of Midcain. But he needed the invaluable poisoned spear, the magical pig-skin, the steeds and the rest. So he sent a druidical spell after them that caused them to forget the cooking-spit and the three shouts on the hill which would complete the fine. In addition to this, the spell filled their hearts with a passionate longing for their own land again, so with unbounded joy they told 'Wave-sweeper' to bear them back to Erin, and to their father Turenn, and to the warriors in Tara of the Kings, where songs would be sung in praise of their deeds until the end of time.

Great indeed was their joy when they saw the grey back of Ben Eader against the western sky, and greater still was it when the prow of 'Wave-sweeper' grounded on the pebbly beach at the Boyne, and they felt the soil of Erin under their feet again. They stood still for a moment to breathe in the gentle Irish air and to let the sight of the bright streams and the heathery slopes of Meath soothe their eyes once more. Then, collecting their treasures, they made straight for Tara, where the High King was holding an assembly.

In Tara the High King and all the noblest warriors of the country welcomed them royally, praising them for the valour of their deeds and rejoicing with them that the blood feud between them and Lugh would, from that day, be at an end for ever.

Meanwhile Lugh, hearing of their return, had slipped off from Tara, and waited at some distance, arrayed in all his arms of valour. Word was sent to him that the Sons of Turenn had returned and had brought the eric with them.

'Have them pay it over to the High King,' said Lugh.

The eric was paid to the High King, and Lugh returned to Tara. Then Brian spoke to Lugh, saying:

'We have paid the blood fine on Kian, O Lugh.'

But Lugh answered:

'It is a good payment indeed for anyone who has been killed, but the blood fine of Kian is not here complete, and you have pledged yourselves not to leave anything out. Where is the cooking-spit of the Faery women of Finchory? And you have not given the three shouts on the Hill of Midcain.'

When the three Sons of Turenn heard this they fell to the ground in a swoon, and then when they recovered they went sadly back to the house of their father, their heads bowed with grief and dismay. They told him with sorrow of all the trials they had endured to get the eric for Lugh, and of the trick that Lugh had played on them in the end. That night they spent with Turenn, and when the morning came they went back to their boat. Eithne and their father accompanied them, and great was their sorrow to see them go.

As their boat bore them away out to sea they looked back at the shape of Ireland growing dim behind them, and there was no hope in their hearts of ever seeing it again, for now it was clear to them that it was not compensation for killing his father that Lugh wanted, but to bring about their destruction only.

For three months they sailed hither and thither on the green, storm-tossed sea, and they could not find any trace of the island of Finchory where the Faery women lived who had the cooking-spit. Then at last Brian decided to put on his water dress and search for the island in the depths of the sea. Leaping over the side of the boat, he left his brothers in 'Wave-sweeper', and for two long weeks he searched the green depths, and at last he came on the island, half-way down to the bed of the ocean, with water under it and over it and around it.

Here among gardens of sea-flowers, tinkling like bells, he found a company of red-haired maidens working gold embroidery around jewels that winked and glinted in the under-water sunlight. There were three times fifty of them, and they sang sweetly as they plied their needles. They looked at Brian as he walked down the hall towards the cooking-spit, but no one spoke. Then, as he seized the spit from the side of the massive hearth, they broke into a ripple of laughter, and one of them said:

'You may carry it away with you, Brian, as a reward for your daring, for bold is your deed in taking it; for even if your two brothers were here to help you, the weakest of us could overcome all three of you.'

Then Brian went back to his brothers in the boat, having thanked the maidens for their cooking-spit, and they lost no time in making for the Hill of Midcain, on which they were to give the three shouts.

When they reached the hill, Midcain himself, the guardian of the hill, came towards them and demanded to know what their business was on his territory.

'We have come to give three shouts on this hill,' said Brian, 'in fulfilment of an eric.'

'I am under bonds never to allow anyone to raise a shout on my hill,' said Midcain.

'Then let our swords speak,' said Brian, and they both drew, and rushed on each other with the fury of two lions, and hard and fierce was the combat, till at last Brian drove his blade through the heart of Midcain, and he fell dead on his own hillside.

Then the three Sons of Midcain came out to fight the three Sons of Turenn, and never before was there such a deadly contest fought between any group of warriors. Now they fought with the ferocity of hungry lions, and then with the wildness of forest boars, and all the time with the staying power of angry bears, till the grass under their feet was a carpet of red blood and the wounds in their bodies were so big that a wood-pigeon could fly out through the two sides of any of them. But the end of it was the three Sons of Midcain fell dead one after the other, and soon after them the three Sons of Turenn fell to the ground more dead than alive from the severity of their wounds.

After some time Brian remembered that they had not done that for which they came, the fulfilment of Lugh's eric, the three shouts on the hill. He raised himself on his elbow and he spoke to his brothers:

'How is it with you, my dear brothers?'

'We are near death,' they answered.

'Let us rise up, then,' said Brian, 'and give three shouts on the hill, for I see the signs of death coming on us.'

Then he dragged himself up, and raising his two brothers with an arm around each, while blood flowed continuously from their wounds, they raised their voices, and with their dying breath gave the three shouts on the Hill of Midcain that Lugh had demanded of them. And so the last of Kian's blood fine was paid, and they fell back exhausted.

After resting for a while, Brian dragged his brothers down to the boat and laid them carefully inside, and lying there between life and death the three Sons of Turenn were borne back to Erin. After journeying over the waves for a long time like this, Brian put up his head and looked over the sea to the west.

'I see Ben Eader, Dun Turenn, and Tara of the Kings, my brothers,' he said gently to them.

The dying brothers opened their eyes when they heard this, and asked him to raise their heads on his breast so that they might get one last glimpse of the land of Erin. 'And then,' they said, 'we care not whether we live or die after that.'

Brian then raised them up, and they saw the furzy brow of Ben Eadar, and the gentle watered plain of the Boyne, and their father's dun near Tara. Then 'Wave-sweeper', instead of grounding at the beach by the mouth of the Boyne, carried them gently and swiftly over land, and did not stop till it brought them to the door of Dun Turenn. Their father came out to meet them with all haste, and he saw, with one look, that the life was only barely in them. Then Brian spoke to him and said:

'Go, my dear father, and take the cooking-spit to Lugh at Tara, and tell him that we have given the three shouts on the Hill of Midcain, and that the eric for Kian is now paid in full, and beg him to lend us the magic pig-skin, so that we may heal our wounds, for there is no cause left now that he should still punish us. And,' he added, as with his dying breath, 'make haste, O my father, for the life that is in us flickers like a rush-light, or you may not find us alive before you on your return.'

Then with all speed Turenn went to Lugh and besought him to give him the pig-skin to save the lives of his sons. Lugh, while Turenn spoke, looked into the distance across the Plain of Muirthemne and was silent. Then after some time he spoke and this is what he said:

'Thy sons have paid the blood-fine for Kian, and in paying it they have fought many a valiant fight, and performed deeds that bards and minstrels will sing to kings and noble companies until the end of time, and now that they have come to their deaths with such valour and renown, to live on after this would be a poor thing.'

When Brian heard from his father that Lugh would not grant them the loan of the healing pig-skin he went and laid himself down between his two brothers, and they put their arms around each other, and life went out of the three of them at the same instant. Then Turenn, kneeling down beside them, kissed each of his sons in turn, and then fell dead over them, for his heart was broken with grief. Eithne, his daughter, then buried them in the one grave, and composed a sorrowful lay over them. And so ends the tale of 'The Quest of the Sons of Turenn' that the bards have named 'One of the Three Sorrows of Story-telling'.

## II

## MIDIR AND ETAIN

Long ago in Erin, when the people of Dana were defeated by the Milesians, they had to go into the hills and mountains, where they built themselves vast palaces inside the hills. Their underground country was a land of the Ever Young where all was beauty, and they knew not death or sorrow. Sometimes they came out and took a mortal lover, and had glorious children, but they always went back again to their own people.

Now, one of the Faery princes, called Midir the Proud, lived on Slieve Callary, a hill outside Dublin. He had a wife named Fuamnach, but his eye fell one day on a beautiful maiden, called Etain, and he fell in love with her and made her his wife.

In a short time Fuamnach became jealous of Etain, whose beauty was so famous throughout the land that 'as fair as Etain' was the highest praise any woman could get. So Fuamnach went to a druid and asked his help to rid herself of her rival. By their magic art they changed Etain into a butterfly, and then they raised a tempest that blew her out of Midir's palace, and buffeted her up and down the country for seven long years.

Now, on the River Boyne, a little north of Dublin, Angus of the Birds, the Irish god of love, had his palace. Four bright birds hovered for ever around his head, and these were said to be his kisses, and when they sang, love was immediately born in the hearts of those who heard them.

It happened that a chance gust blew Etain in through one of the windows of the faery palace of Angus, and as people of the Faery can never be hidden from one another, Angus recognized Etain in the guise of the wind-tossed butterfly. Though he could not release her from all the spells that Fuamnach had put on her, he could remove the spell from dusk till dawn, so that during that time she regained her shape as a beautiful maiden, and Angus kept her in his palace always, and gave her his love. He built a pleasant sunny house for her, bedecked with flowers, sweet-smelling and honey-laden, for the day-time when she was a butterfly, and he put invisible walls around it so that nobody could see her.

After some happy years with Angus, Etain was to know misfortune again, for Fuamnach found out where she was. Once more she sent a tempest after her that blew her around Ireland as before, and she was in great misery.

Now all this time Midir was searching for Etain in every corner of the land, but in no place did he find a trace of his beautiful bride.

At last it happened that she was blown in through the windows of the palace of the King of Leinster, who was holding a feast. Etain fluttered up on to the roof-beam over the royal throng, where she rested for a while, but after a few seconds she fell off the beam, and dropped into the goblet of wine that the Queen was just drinking. The Queen drank her down with the wine, and at the end of nine months she was born again as a king's daughter and apparently as a mortal child. She was named Etain, and in course of time she grew up to be as beautiful as she had ever been.

At this time the High King of Ireland was without a wife, and the nobles were urging him to take one. 'For if you do not do so, we will not bring our wives to the Royal Assembly at Tara,' they told him.

One day, shortly after this petition, the High King was out hunting, and came on Etain with her maidens sunning themselves in the meadows. The High King wooed her and made her his wife, and they were very happy until the Great Assembly at Tara.

On the first day of the Assembly Etain was out on the green watching the races and the games when she saw a rider on a milk-white steed coming towards her. As he drew near she noted the royal purple cloak blowing behind him in the breeze, and the hair on his head that was as golden as the irises that bloom in the May-time streams. No one of her companions could see him or hear the invitation that he gave her to come with him back to the land of Faery, the country of the Ever Young.

This rider with the golden hair and the flowing purple cloak was Midir the Proud, and after many years' searching without cease he had at last found Etain, the beautiful young bride who had been spirited away from him, where to and by whom he did not know. But now, alas, Etain did not remember him, knew nothing of their love, and would not go back to the land of Faery with him without her husband's, the High King's, consent. Midir knew he would never get the King's consent, so he left her sadly.

Shortly after this the High King was at his window one day, when he saw a rider on a white horse and wearing a purple cloak come riding across the plain. He drew up and asked the High King to play a game of chess with him. The King consented, and Midir the Proud, for it was he, took out a gold-wrought chess-board with jewelled pieces, and they began to play. The High King won the first game, and the second, and Midir paid the King's stake and asked for a third game.

They played for the third time, and this time Midir the Proud won.

'What is your stake?' asked the High King.

'My stake is that I obtain one kiss from Etain,' said Midir.

The King was silent for a while on hearing this; then he spoke and said: 'One month from now you may come back, and what you ask shall be granted.'

Now, since the meeting with Midir on the Plain of the Assembly Etain began to dream of her former life among the Faery. Little by little she began to recall all she had forgotten, her love for Midir returned, and she pined and fretted day by day for her Faery lover and for her own country, the Land of Faery. Midir, too, was pining for Etain, and he hovered unseen around the High King's palace until the month was up and he could claim his stake.

At last the appointed day came, and the High King mustered all his armed hosts, and placed them around his palace, and the city of Tara was like a forest of steel with their blue spears.

Inside the palace the High King and his nobles and chosen warriors sat at the feast, and Etain was handing around the wine, when suddenly in the middle of the banqueting hall Midir appeared, and he was more glorious and more beautiful than ever.

Holding his spear in his left hand, with his right arm he encircled Etain, and then lightly and gently they were wafted up in the air and out through a top window.

The alarm was raised, and each man put his hand on his weapons, but when the King and his nobles rushed out of the door all they could see were two white swans circling in the starry sky over the palace.

## III

## THE CHILDREN OF LIR

*(The second sorrow of story-telling)*

Now, it happened that a race of people called the Milesians invaded Ireland at this time with the idea of taking the country for themselves. They fought a war with the People of Dana, and in two bloody battles, on the Plain of Moytura, the invaders defeated the People of Dana, and so put an end to the reign of the gods in Ireland for evermore.

The Milesians now divided the country into two equal parts, an upper half, above the ground, and the lower half, below the ground. They themselves took the upper half, the surface of the earth, and they gave the territory under the ground to the People of Dana. So the vanquished gods retired underground, going into the hills and earth-mounds of the country, where they built themselves vast palaces sparkling with jewels and precious stones, and there continued to live a life of wondrous beauty. It was a land where time did not pass away, a land of eternal summer, where no one grew old, and where men and women were divinely beautiful:

Delightful land beyond all dreams
Beyond what seems to us most fair,
Rich fruits abound the bright year round
And flowers are found of hue most rare.

As soon as they settled in their new home the De Danaans came together to choose a king, and the one of their choice was Bov the Red. Now, Bov the Red was beloved of all, and everybody settled down peacefully under him with one exception, and that was Lir, the father of Manannan Mac Lir, the sea-god. Lir, offended at not being chosen himself, withdrew to his palace at Shee Finnehy, the Stronghold of the White Field, under a large hill in the present County Armagh, and from that day on never attended at Court or showed any mark of respect to the new King.

After some time Bov the Red, who was a king of great wisdom and of a noble nature, sent for Lir and offered him one of his three foster-daughters in marriage, in order to draw him back into the circle of his friends once more. Lir was touched by the King's forgiveness, and no sooner did he get Bov's message than he set out next day for the royal palace on the shores of Lough Derg, on the Shannon, to swear fealty at last to Bov.

When Lir arrived at Lough Derg he and his company of fifty were welcomed with great splendour by the King, and a banquet was prepared at once for their reception. During the banquet the three foster-daughters of Bov, Eve, Eva and Alva, sat with their foster-mother, and the King invited Lir to take his choice of the three.

'They are all equally beautiful,' said Lir, 'but I shall choose the eldest, since she must be the wisest, according to her age.'

So Lir and Eve were married that day, and after two weeks of feasting and rejoicing Lir brought his bride home to Shee Finnehy. After some time a pair of twins were born to them—a daughter and a son, whom they named Finola and Aed. Lir delighted in his wife, and in his beautiful children, and his happiness knew no bounds. A year or two passed, and Eve bore him another pair of twins, this time two sons, and they were named Fiacra and Conn, but alas, she died soon after their birth. Lir mourned her deeply, and it is said that he would have died of grief if the love he had for his children had not turned his mind away from the loss of his wife.

When news of the death of Eve reached Bov the Red he and his household were greatly grieved by the loss of their foster-daughter, but they mourned, too, for the sorrow of Lir. As soon as the mourning was over the King sent messengers to Lir to come and take his second daughter, Eva, for his wife.

After due time Lir went again to Bov's palace, and married Eva the second daughter, and brought her back with him to Shee Finnehy, where she took over the care of his household and of his four children. Eva tended Lir's children with loving care, and they in turn gave her great affection, and once more Lir knew great happiness. His love for his four beautiful children and the pleasure they gave him grew greater every day as he watched them grow. So fond was he of them that he had them sleep in a chamber near his own, so that they should never be far from him, and in the early morning he used to rise from his bed as soon as they were awake, to talk to them, to tell them old tales and to pet and fondle them. He also took them on frequent visits to their grandfather the King, so that Bov the Red knew and loved them almost as much as did their own father. And indeed so it was with all the De Danaan nobles, for nowhere in all the land were there four such beautiful and lovable children as Finola, Aed, Fiacra and Conn.

Now, when everyone seemed most happy and all was joy and peace in the household of Lir, a feeling of jealousy against the children suddenly entered into the heart of Eva. It seemed to her that the regard and love that they got from Lir and his friends, the nobles of the De Danaans, should be hers by right, and even her own foster-father Bov seemed to prize his grandchildren so highly that he had no longer any thoughts for her. Little by little hate against them began to grow in her heart, so, feigning an illness, she lay in bed for a year, during which time she imagined herself neglected by all, and her hate of the children grew day by day, till at last she could not bear the sight of them, and she began to make a plot to rid herself of their presence.

So one day, feeling that she could not bear them about her any longer, she rose from her bed and ordered her chariot to be yoked. Then she called the children to her and told them that she was taking them to visit her father Bov the Red at Lough Derg.

Finola, either having noticed the change in Eva's feeling towards her and her brothers or through having the evil in her stepmother's heart revealed to her in a dream, had a suspicion that Eva meant to do them harm, and so refused to go. But so strong was the knot that bound her to her fate that she allowed herself to be persuaded, and her three brothers Aed, Fiacra and Conn took their seats beside Eva in the chariot, and they started off south towards the lake in the Shannon.

When they had gone some distance away from Lir's palace, Eva stopped the chariot and tried to persuade the servants to kill the children, saying:

'They have robbed me of Lir's love and of my father's kind affection. Kill them,' she told them, 'and all I possess shall be yours.'

But the servants drew back in horror of the madness that possessed her, and chiding her for the deed she contemplated, they warned her:

'Fearful is the wicked deed you ask of us, O Eva, and evil will surely fall on thee for even having thought of it.'

On then they went once more till they came to Lake Derravaragh, in the middle of Ireland. Here she ordered her company to alight and to unyoke the horses. And leading the four children to the lakeside, she told them to bathe while the horses were resting. Timidly they took off their garments and waded in over the rocky shore, and

Eva, seeing them in the water, struck them one by one with a druid's wand and changed them into four beautiful, snow-white swans. Then, in the hearing of her servants, she spoke their doom:

> 'Here on Derravaragh's lonely wave
> For many a year to be your watery home,
> No power of Lir or druid can now ye save
> From endless wandering on the lonely foam.'

As they listened to their fate the four swans looked with sad and frightened faces at their stepmother, and then Finola said:

'Why, O Eva, have you done such an evil deed to us, who loved you and whom you loved? We gave you no cause, and your deed will surely be punished by a fate worse than ours.'

As Eva listened to Finola's plaint the raging jealousy began to die in her heart, and, as it did, all the horror of the deed she had done came over her. But she could not now undo it. Then she declared the full term of their enchantment:

'Three hundred years you will spend on Lake Derravaragh, three hundred on the Sea of Moyle, between Erin and Alban, and three hundred on Inish Glora, on the Western Sea. And you will keep the shape of swans until a prince from the North will take in marriage a princess from the South, and till you hear the voice of the Christian bell bringing the light of the new faith over the land.' And, trying to lessen the hardship she had put on them, she said:

'I will leave to you the power of human speech, and I will give you the power of making sweet, plaintive music that will soothe the mind and hearts of all who will listen to it, and you shall in all things, except in shape, have your own natures.'

Then, ordering her steed to be yoked once more, she drove south to Lough Derg, to the house of Bov the Red, and left the four white swans on the lonely moorland lake.

Great was the disappointment of Bov when Eva arrived

without the grandchildren who were so dear to his heart. Greatly, too, was he astonished when she told him that Lir would not permit the children to come with her on this visit to the house of their grandfather.

'Lir no longer has friendship in his heart towards thee,' she told him, 'and so he would not trust his children under thy roof.'

'This surely cannot be,' said the old King, 'for he knows I love those children as if they were my own.'

Secretly and with all speed, for he was greatly puzzled, Bov sent messengers back to Shee Finnehy to ask about the children and to request that they be sent to him as soon as possible.

When Lir received the message, telling him that his children had not arrived with Eva at the palace of Bov, he became greatly worried, and ordered his chariot to be yoked without delay, and he set out for Lough Derg to see for himself what had become of them. After some hours of hard driving he came to Lough Derravaragh, and there he saw the four white swans swimming majestically towards him, singing sweet, sad music as they came. Lir caused his chariot to be drawn up close to the shore while he gazed with silent wonder at the strange sight of the swans singing and conversing with human voices. After a while Finola swam still closer to him, and said in sweet, low tone, so low that he had to bend down his ear to hear:

'You see before thee, O Lir, thy four beloved children in the shape of four white swans, turned from their human form for ever by the hand of their stepmother, Eva, through jealousy of thy love for them.'

Hearing this, Lir and his people raised three mournful cries of grief and lamentation, but Finola bade them to cease mourning for them, for it was of no avail, and to comfort them she told them that Eva had left them their human wits:

'We will keep our speech and our reason, and we also have the power to chant music so exquisite that it brings happiness and content to all who hear it.'

Then Lir asked the swans to come back home to Shee Finnehy, where they could live among their friends and have the love and devotion of all.

'Alas,' Finola answered, 'it is not permitted for us to leave this lake for three hundred years, and from here we must go to spend three hundred on the stormy Sea of Moyle, and three hundred more on Inish Glora in the Western Sea.'

Lir and his followers were now sorely grieved, but Finola and her brothers sang them their sweet strains, and peace and calm crept into their hearts, and they fell into a gentle sleep.

Next morning Lir rose early and drove at once to Bov's palace to seek out Eva. The minute Bov saw Lir he reproached him for not permitting Eva to bring the children with her. Lir looked at him in astonishment and said:

'Alas, it is not I who prevented their coming, but your own foster-daughter, Eva, the very sister of their mother, who through her spells has changed them into four swans, and in that form they now swim on Lake Derravaragh.'

The King looked at his daughter and saw the evil shining in her eyes. Gently and sadly he upbraided her, and told her that she must be made to suffer till the end of time for the evil thing she had done. Then, taking a druidical wand and raising it over her, he changed her into a demon of the air.

Flapping her wings and uttering a piercing shriek, she flew upwards out of sight into the dark clouds, and there she lives, still a demon of the air, it is said, to this day.

Then Lir and Bov the Red and a number of the De Danaan nobles drove in their chariots to the shores of Derravaragh, where they encamped so that they might be near the swans and keep them company. And so, with their friends near them to comfort and help them, the swans lived on Lake Derravaragh for three hundred years. They spent the day conversing and listening to old tales, and the night singing sweet music that soothed every troubled heart and brought peace and gentle sleep to all. So the time passed pleasantly till at last their term on Derravaragh was over, and they had to leave for the Sea of Moyle. Finola called her three brothers to her and said to them:

'My grief it is, my dear brothers, that we have come to the end of our time on Lake Derravaragh, and tomorrow at dawn we must leave it for ever and go northward to the stormy Sea of Moyle.'

Sad indeed were Aed, Fiacra and Conn at hearing this, for they had been almost as happy on the smooth, sheltered lake of Derravaragh, among all their friends, as they had been in their home at Shee Finnehy. But now leaving it for the cold and stormy Sea of Moyle, far away from their beloved father and their dear friends, where their only company would be the shrieking sea-gulls and the cold fishy seals, they were downcast indeed. And as the lake grew white in the dawn-light the four swans gathered before Lir's encampment to speak to him for the last time, and Finola started to sing a sad, sweet lay, and her brothers joined in. Then the four swans spread their wings and, still singing, rose from the water, and crossed the calm bosom of the lake, and turned north-east for the Sea of Moyle.

Sad and miserable was the plight of the four swans that night on the Sea of Moyle. As they came to rest on its storm-tossed waters they looked around them, but no sign of friend or human did they see, only the grey heaving waste of water stretching off to break in the distance against black, unfriendly rocks.

Many lonely and desolate days and nights were they destined to pass in this inhuman region, but no night in all the three hundred years they were to spend on the Sea of Moyle was as bad as the one they spent during their first winter there. That day, a short time after their coming, as evening came on, great masses of black clouds gathered over their heads, the waves grew black and hissed and boiled around them, and soon snow began to fall in blinding shafts. Seeing the storm coming, Finola spoke to her brothers:

'Dear brothers, a night of storm such as we have never known in Erin is nearly upon us, and it is certain that we shall be blown and buffeted by the angry wind and sea, and separated from one another. So let us name a place to meet again when the tempest is past.'

Then she and her brothers agreed that when the wind and storm died down they would all go to the rock of Carricknarone, a rock which they knew, and where they spent much of their time. Now, as darkness came on, the lightning flashed and the thunder rolled around them, and as the wind rose to greater fury the sea heaved itself into cliff-like waves. They soon lost sight of each other, and were blown many miles apart. At last when morning dawned, and the sea grew calm once more, Finola made for Carricknarone as quickly as she could to meet and comfort her brothers after their night of hardship.

But alas, when she reached the rock there was not a sign of one of them to be seen, and even when she climbed the rock, and looked out all around her on the wide face of the sea, still there was not a trace of them on any side. Overcome with grief, she began to sing a sad lament for her brothers and for her own fate at being left alone in this desolate region. But she had only just finished her lay when up swam Conn in answer to her call. His feathers were bedraggled, his head was drooping with weariness, and one of his wings was broken, but she welcomed him with joy and she took heart again. Soon after this Fiacra, faint with cold, came into sight, and he was soon followed by Aed. Finola put one of her brothers under each of her wings, and she placed Conn under the feathers of her breast.

So with many hardships the three hundred years of the Sea of Moyle passed at last, and one day Finola called Conn, Fiacra and Aed to her and said:

'We must leave this place, dear brothers, for our time here has come to an end. We must fly westward now, to Inish Glora in the Western Sea, and on our way we shall visit again Shee Finnehy and see once more our beloved father and our dear friends.'

Her brothers were greatly rejoiced to hear this, and with light hearts the four swans rose in the air and flew south towards Shee Finnehy, the palace of Lir. But when they came over the rich plains of Armagh and looked eagerly down, they could not make out any sign of Lir's palace. Circling high and wide they searched the land for any trace of his dwelling, but in vain. Then they alighted on the very earth mound under which Lir's dwelling had been, and though they walked around its grassy slopes and ramparts, all they could find were a few walls overgrown with nettles and docks, and the only sound they could hear was the wind whining in the elders and nettles, that were growing where the great door into the banqueting hall once stood. Coming together on the ruins of their once loved home the four swans now began to sing a lament:

'What meaneth this sad, this fearful change,
That withers my heart with woe?
The house of my father all joyless and lone,
Its halls and its gardens with weeds overgrown,
A dreadful and strange overthrow!

No conquering heroes, no hounds for the chase,
No shields in array on its walls,
No bright silver goblets, no gay cavalcades,
No youthful assemblies, no high-born maids,
To brighten its desolate halls!

An omen of sadness—the home of our youth
All ruined, deserted and bare.
Alas for the chieftain, the gentle and brave;
His glories and sorrows are stilled in the grave,
And we left to live in despair!

From ocean to ocean, from age unto age,
We have lived to the fulness of time;
Through a life such as men never heard of we've passed
In suffering and sorrow our doom has been cast,
By our stepmother's pitiless crime!'

That night the swans stayed among the ruins of their ancient home and sadly chanted their sweet music, but on the coming of dawn they left Shee Finnehy and faced west for Inish Glora, where they came down on a small lake. Here they continued to sing their songs and their lays, and the birds from the mainland, hearing them, gathered around them in flocks to listen, for never before had they heard any music so beautiful. And they came in such flocks that the lake came to be called the Lake of the Birds, and so it is named to this day.

It was at this time that Holy Patrick had come to Ireland and was telling the people of the One True God and of Christ, His Son. And he was going up and down the country preaching to the people and building churches and monasteries for them. One of his followers, who was called Kemoc, came to Inish Glora and built a church there. On the morning after his coming the children of Lir were awakened by the sound of his bell ringing for Matins at dawn. And as the strange sound of the bell came over the waters of the lake it greatly frightened the four swans, for it was unlike the sound of tympan or lyre or harp, or any other musical sound they had ever heard. Then Finola spoke to her brothers of the bell saying:

'That sound that affrights you, my brothers, is the voice of the Christian bell, and it tells us that the end of our suffering is near, and Eva's enchantment will soon have passed away.'

Then the four swans began to sing a hymn of gladness. The sweet strains of the fairy music floated across the silent lake, and in through the reedy walls of Kemoc's cell, where he was kneeling at Matins. Holy Kemoc now went down to the lake-shore and spoke to the swans, and asked them if they were the Children of Lir, who were famous throughout the land for their beautiful singing. They told him they were indeed the Children of Lir, and told the saint of the spell put on them by their stepmother nearly a thousand years before. Kemoc then bade them to put themselves under his care, 'for it is laid down that it is in this place you are to be freed from your enchantment.'

So the swans came ashore and willingly went with the holy man. He brought them to his house, where they lived with him from that day on, and he told them of the One True God and of Christ, His Son, and they joined with him in his prayers and devotions. And so at last a heavenly peace fell on the Children of Lir, and great was the happiness they found with Holy Kemoc in the little island in the Lake of the Birds.

But their trials were not yet over, for it was ordained by Eva that her spell would not be broken till the princess from the South married a prince from the North. Now, it happened that at this time Decca, daughter of Finnin, King of Munster, had just married Largnen, a king who ruled over Connacht. Word was brought to Decca of the beautiful singing swans who lived in the Lake of the Birds in her husband's kingdom, and she was determined to have them for her own. She asked Largnen to have the swans brought to her, but Largnen did not wish to ask them of Kemoc until forced by Decca, who threatened to go back to her father in Munster unless her wish was granted. Largnen then sent a messenger requesting Holy Kemoc to give him the swans for the Queen, but Kemoc refused to give them up.

Largnen grew very angry at this refusal and went himself to the Holy Kemoc and demanded the swans. The saint again refused, and the King, now furious, went into the little church where Kemoc had put the swans for safety, and dragged them from the altar to take them to the Queen. But he had gone but three paces from the church door when the feathery plumage fell from the swans, and they regained their human shape. Finola was transformed into a frail, white-faced old woman, and her three brothers into three feeble old men, grey-haired, bony and wrinkled.

Seeing them, the King fled in fear and horror, but Kemoc's bitter denunciation followed him as he went. The children of Lir called out then to the saint to come and baptise them, for they felt that death was near, and Finola asked him to bury them in one grave:

'For as I often sheltered my brothers under my wings when we were swans, so let us be placed in one grave, side by side, Conn standing at one side of me and Fiacra at the other and Aed before my face.'

Then they died peacefully, and Holy Kemoc laid them side by side in the one grave, and he raised an earth mound over them and put a tombstone on it with their names engraved in ogham.

# *IN THE TIME OF CUCHULLIN*

# I

# HOW CONOR MAC NESSA BECAME KING OF ULSTER

*A Foretale to The Cattle Raid of Cooley*

CONOR MAC NESSA was the King of Ulster at the time of its greatest glory—that of the famous champion, Cuchullin, and of the Red Branch Knights whose deeds of valour made Ulster powerful and feared by the men of Erin.

Conor Mac Nessa, as his name tells, was the son of Nessa, and she had been the wife of Fachtna the Giant, King of Ulster. When Fachtna died, Fergus, his half-brother, became king, for Conor was but a youth. Now, Nessa was still beautiful, and Fergus Mac Roy fell in love with her and wished to make her his wife. But Nessa would consent only on one condition—that Fergus should let Conor, her son, reign for one year as King of Ulster, so that his sons and his grandsons could say they were the sons and grandsons of a king.

Fergus was kind-hearted and easy-going, and as he was most anxious to please Nessa, he consented to this condition and gave up the throne to Conor for one year. During that year Nessa instructed and guided her son so that in everything he did he pleased the nobles of the province. She gave him gold to spend in feasting the Court and the nobles, and to distribute among the people so that all should say there never was a more liberal king in Ulster. She also guided him in matters of governing the country so that he always did the wise and just thing in handling the affairs of state, and so Nessa brought it about that during that year the people of Ulster were more prosperous and content than at any time anyone could remember. Everyone said that this happiness and prosperity was all due to the wise rule of the youthful Conor, and when the time came for Fergus to take back the kingship, the nobles and people banded together to keep Conor as their king. For, they said, Fergus cared less for the kingship than Conor, since he gave it up to gain a wife. So Fergus, the gay warrior poet, the pleasure-lover, who really loved the chase and the ale-feast more than the toils and cares of kingship, was content to let things be, and Conor remained King of Ulster, and Fergus stayed on at his court loyal and content for many a year. But Conor was cruel and treacherous, and after some years Fergus quarrelled bitterly with him on account of his slaying the three Sons of Usnach. Fergus at this time led a rebellion against Conor, but, being defeated, sought refuge in Connacht, where many of the best warriors of the Red Branch went with him, and offered their swords to Queen Maeve, Conor's most powerful enemy.

When Fergus left Ulster, Conor lost one of his best fighting men and suffered a great loss to his power and warlike strength, for next to Cuchullin, there was no champion in Ulster that could compare with Fergus. It was said of him that his strength was that of seven hundred men, that he was as tall as a giant, and that he would eat seven hogs, seven deer and seven kine and drink seven vats at one meal. He had a famous sword that had been brought to him out of Faery. It was said to be as long as a weaver's beam, and that when he raised it to strike a blow it stretched out and became as long as a rainbow. It is no wonder that Conor feared for the safety of his province when such a fighter as Fergus went over to his enemy.

The first thing that Conor did was to double the number of the Red Branch Knights, so as to increase his warlike strength and to make Ulster so strong that Maeve or his other enemies would be afraid to attack it. The Red Branch Knights were a body of champion warriors, chosen for their strength and bravery and specially trained in the art of warlike deeds. They were part of the household troops of the King of Ulster, and Conor had a special house built for them within his own grounds in Emain Macha. Every summer, too, he brought large bodies of young men from all over the province to have them drilled and trained under his own eye in Emain Macha, and their captains he feasted in the great banqueting hall of the royal palace.

Conor then turned to the youth of Ulster and started a military training-school for young boys, the sons of his nobles and chieftains, where they would be taught games and all kinds of athletic feats, so that they should grow up strong and brave like their fathers, and find a place among the champions of the Red Branch. Conor took much interest in this boy-corps, and it is said that he gave them lands near his own palace in which to practice their games and their feats, and that he spent a portion of every day watching their training. According as they gained in strength and skill the King gave each one a complete war outfit: a small spear, a short sword and a light shield suitable to his age and strength, but just as complete as the equipment of any of his men warriors.

So it was that Conor tried to make Ulster supreme over all the other provinces of Erin, and so well did he succeed that no one dared to attack it except at the times when a strange magical sickness seized the King, his warriors and all the Knights of the Red Branch. Now, this strange sickness was the result of a spell put on them by the angry goddess, Macha, whom Conor had mocked. It happened that, some time before, Macha had come to Ulster out of the faery mound and had fallen in love with an Ulster farmer. She went to live with him on his farm, helped him to work it and was in every way a good, attentive wife, though she was a goddess and surpassed in beauty, strength and swiftness of foot all the other women of Ulster. Now Conor, hearing her praised, grew jealous and envious, and scoffed at her in public, and she became so angry that she cursed the men of Ulster and told them that every year at the coming of winter a sickness would seize them with dreadful pain, weakness and deep slumber. She also told them that at a time of their greatest danger, when a powerful enemy would be over-running their borders, they would be seized by their pangs, and that each warrior would not have as much strength as a newly born child.

# II

# THE CATTLE RAID OF COOLEY

## I

## *The Pillow Talk*

MAEVE, the beautiful and proud Queen of Connacht, sat with her husband, Ailell, and each boasted of having riches and treasures greater than the other. They spoke of their flocks and their herds, their hirelings and bondswomen, their golden torcs and goblets, and their vessels of silver and white bronze. They had them brought and set before them, and they compared and counted them all down to the humblest of their goods—the mugs, vats and iron urns, the brewers' troughs and keeves—and in all things Maeve was equal to her husband. Among Maeve's sheep was a famous ram, but Ailell was able to show one that compared well with him. Maeve had a prize boar, but Ailell had another. Maeve pointed to a notable thoroughbred, but Ailell had one to match him. And so the counting and comparing of their goods showed them equal in all things but one—Ailell had a famous white-horned bull among his herds, and Maeve had none to put against him. So, on account of this, Maeve thought the value of her whole property was not worth as much as a pin, since she lacked that one thing that would make her equal to her husband. Straightway she called for Mac Roth, the Herald, and ordered him to find out where in the whole land of Erin could be found for her a bull the equal of Ailell's. Mac Roth told her there was such a bull in the house of Daire Mac Fiachniu, in the Ulster country, and that he was known as 'The Brown Bull of Cooley'. Hearing this, Maeve bade Mac Roth set off at once, and take with him gifts to Daire, and ask for the loan of his Brown Bull for the space of one year.

Mac Roth set out, and taking with him nine servants made for the Dun of Daire with all speed. Reaching it, he presented his gifts, and he and his servants were well received, rushes and fresh sedge being strewn on the floors for them, and delicate meats and heady wines were laid out for their refreshment. In due course Mac Roth asked for the loan of the Brown Bull for his royal mistress, and offered as the loan's fee a piece of land in Connacht equal in size to the land Daire already owned in Ulster, a chariot and thrice seven bondsmaids, fifty heifers, and Maeve's honour and esteem till the day of his death. When Daire heard this offer, it is said that he was so pleased that he bounded about upon his couch with such joy that the seams of the feather tick burst under him. Willingly he agreed to the bargain, and he went off himself to prepare to send the Brown Bull into Connacht.

More and stronger wine was now sent for and set before Mac Roth and Maeve's runners to seal the bond, and as they drank the heady wine, their tongues were loosened, their voices grew loud and they began to argue and vie with the Ulstermen, forgetting the caution that Mac Roth bade them bear in mind. And so the talk and boasting grew louder and louder until one Connachtman's voice, shouting down all others, was heard to say, 'Well it is for Daire that he yields the Brown Bull of Cooley to us by his own will, for had he refused, Queen Maeve and her army would have carried it out of Ulster by force.'

On this being reported to Daire he grew angry, and coming before the Connachtmen he cried out:

'By the gods whom I adore, I swear that, unless by foul means, he shall never now go into Connacht. Let Maeve and Ailell come and take it if they can, but Ulster will prepare to hold the bull.'

Mac Roth and his nine messengers then went back to Maeve and told her that Daire refused the loan of the bull owing to the boasting of one of her runners, drunk with wine. But the proud Queen, waving aside all the Herald's excuses, said:

'By my troth, Mac Roth, there is no need to polish knots over the reason of his refusal, for it was known to all that if the Brown Bull was not given with their will he would be taken without it, and taken he shall be.'

Then Fergus Mac Roy, who sat by Maeve, said that there was every sign of a mighty war to come, over these two bulls; 'For', he said, 'they have been sent by the jealous gods into Erin, to cause destruction and tumult among men.

'Out of the faery places they came,' went on Fergus, 'the White-Horned to Connacht, and the Brown Bull to the herd of Daire of Cooley in the Ulster country. Each bull is enormous in size and has the strength of fifty ordinary bulls. It is said of the Brown that upon his broad back, as he lies quiet at evening time, fifty little boys can play at their games. It is said, too, that if he is angered, his snorting and bellowing are like unto the thunder rolling through the land of Erin, and if any be so bold as to draw nigh to him in his rage, he would trample them fully thirty feet down into the earth. Like a king he is in his pride and splendour,' said Fergus, 'as he marches before his cows, his mighty bull-front raised above the herd, and his horns tipped with gold.'

'In all the land of Erin there is no equal to him in strength, in splendour and in pride,' said Ailell, 'but the White-Horned Bull of Connacht.'

'I would hear more of these messengers of the gods,' Maeve said, turning to Fergus.

'Before they took on the shape of bulls,' said Fergus, 'they came into the land in other forms, but in whatever way they came, they always brought wars and destruction with them. Once they came as two swineherds of the gods, and kept the fairy cattle of the gods of Munster and Connacht, but at that time, too, they stirred up a mighty war, that with killings and burnings ravaged the whole land. Then for two hundred years they lived as two ravens among the race of men, but in the end they tore each other to pieces and died fighting. And now that they have come to earth again it is certain that they will drag the race of men after them to ruin and destruction.'

'It suits us well that we should enter into war at this time,' said Maeve, 'for we are all prepared, Ulster's bravest warriors are on our side, our allies and our hirelings wait on our commands, and Conor and his Red Branch Knights are stricken in their spell sickness.'

So the proud Queen decided to invade Ulster, and calling for her runners and captains of war she sent out messengers to her allies all over the land to come and join her in the war. And daily they began to arrive to swell the muster around her palace at Rathcruachan, companies of men in flowing kilts and long beards from the far south and west, giant-sized warriors from the fat lands of Leinster in the east, and even from Ulster itself there was a company under Fergus Mac Roy, who, while not anxious to fight against their own countrymen, were eager to strike at Conor for his treachery in killing their brave comrades, the three Sons of Usnach. Ailell likewise mustered his forces and called on his allies, and before long the flat land around the royal palace of Maeve was one great warrior camp waiting for the word of the Queen to move off to war.

At night from her palace on a hill over the encampment Maeve looked out and saw the clustering tents of the Men of Erin. It was a goodly army that lay around her ramparts, their camp-fires blackening the stars, and their spears glinting in the firelight. Her spies, too, were coming in from Ulster saying that in all that land there was no hand

K-M

that could lift a spear, for all the warriors of Ulster still lay under the spell of Macha's curse—the spell that the angry goddess had put on Ulster's warriors every year in revenge for Conor's ill-treatment of her.

This surely, then, was the moment for the Men of Erin to set out and take Ulster unaware, when in all the land there was not one to stay their march. But Maeve's druids and wise men held her back until such time as a good omen should come about. The foretellings were not good, and Maeve herself was troubled, for did not Fedelma the Prophetess tell of a young man of Ulster who would mow down many of the Men of Erin, and kill Maeve's bravest champions? And so twenty precious days were spent in watching signs and omens, and in consulting with her druids and wise men, until at last the most learned of all her wizards told of a good augury and a lucky time for setting out.

Then Maeve named Fergus Mac Roy chief scout to the army of the Men of Erin, for he, being an Ulsterman, knew the fords and the trackless ways that lay along the border. She took command of the whole army herself, and, calling for her chariot to be yoked, she drew her sword and entered into it. Then she appeared before her troops, 'a woman beautiful, white-skinned, long cheeked, tall and with yellow hair down to her shoulders', and with her sword brandished over her head, like a veritable goddess of war, she drove around the entire host, to observe their temper and to see in what order they were to march. Then, at her word, the army of the Men of Erin raised a forest of steel over their heads and began their march into Ulster.

## II

# *Cuchullin Keeps the Gap of the North*

When Maeve's army started out on the road to Ulster, Fergus, their chief scout and guide, led them forward. But as he drew near the border and saw his native country out before him, Fergus more and more began to dislike the task that Maeve had set him—of leading the Men of Erin into Ulster. So he started to lead the armies of Maeve astray up and down the country, across rough and boggy tracks to weary them and to waste their time, so that by the evening of the first day they were really not far from where they had started that morning. Fergus also sent secret messages ahead to the Ulster chiefs, and particularly to Cuchullin, whom he loved as a son, telling them of Maeve's coming, and urging them to muster their men and get ready to defend their land.

Maeve soon realized that Fergus was not leading her army to the border by the shortest way, and she charged him with it. But Fergus answered her haughtily:

'I will never lead the Men of Erin against my province. You must get another to guide your troops.'

That night Cuchullin was at Muirthemne with his father when he got the secret warning from Fergus. He ordered

Laegh to prepare his chariot, and, sending his father up to Emain Macha to arouse the King and his Warriors of the Red Branch, he drove off, telling him as he left:

'I will take my stand on the border between Ulster and the Men of Erin and I will keep the Gap of the North against them until the King and the Warriors of the Red Branch will have come out of their sickness. From this day I will so harass and worry the hosts of Maeve that they will wish they had never set forth.'

Next day he drove along the border until he found the track of the Men of Erin. Then he went into a wood and cut down an oak sapling. He pulled it once between his toes to strip it of its twigs and branches, and made it so bare and smooth that it is said that a midge would be hard set to get a footing on it. Then he caught it between his finger-tips and hurled it across the ford, so that it stood up midway in the river. Now, taking a strip of birch bark, he put down on it his name in secret writing and also a warning to the Men of Erin that they were not to come beyond this point, and he tied the strip of bark to the pole. As he was doing this he saw two of Maeve's scouts creep up and stand watching him, concealed in the trees. With one leap Cuchullin fell on them and struck off both their heads. These together with the heads of their charioteers he put on the four prongs of the forked pole he had stuck in the middle of the ford. Then he got the two chariots, and placing in each the two bloody, headless bodies, he turned the horses' heads around and sent them galloping back to the camp of the Men of Erin.

With her own eyes Maeve saw the returning chariots, and then the four dripping, gory heads on the forked pole. This, she felt sure, must be the work of a large company of warriors, and fearing that the armies of Ulster were stealing up on her, she sent for Fergus to question him.

Fergus looked at the pole and read Cuchullin's message for Maeve. But the haughty Queen was loath to believe that any one Ulster warrior could deal at one time with four of her soldiers. Fergus then told her that Cuchullin was no ordinary warrior, and warned her that of his strength and skill in war she would have more proof before many days were at an end.

As Fergus spoke, Maeve bethought herself of the prophecy of Fadelma, the woman from the Faery, about the youthful Cuchullin who would mow down many of the Men of Erin, and the haughty Queen became uneasy. But she did not wish that Fergus should see she was afraid of Cuchullin, so she called on her captains to push on into Ulster by forced marches. In this way she thought to put Cuchullin behind her, and to subdue Ulster while the King and his warriors were still in their sickness.

So on they went, the great host of the Men of Erin, travelling over rough country, and now at times the snow was up to the hubs of their chariot wheels. But no matter how quickly they went, or how long their marches, Cuchullin seemed to be on the path before them, or on their right flank or on their left, picking off their men in twos and threes, killing their scouts and harassing their rear. Never once did anyone catch sight of him, and all they heard of him was the sound of his sling sending stone after stone whistling through the air over their heads all night long as they tried to sleep in their camp.

At last he so terrified them that the scouts refused to go out except in large numbers, and Maeve herself got sorely nervous. So once again Maeve sent for Fergus, and bade him tell Ailell and her captains of war as they sat in council all he knew of this warrior and his warlike skill.

In the dark of the winter's night as Fergus made his way to the royal quarters no torch or fire lit up the encampment of the Men of Erin. No word of song or sound of lute gave even a hint of the resting army. Every tent-flap was closed and every voice was lowered, for all knew that outside the rim of the encampment a dangerous foe lurked, and was watching to strike. Who that foe was, and what was his strength in numbers, no one could say for certain, but a hundred rumours were running through the camp of a vast Ultonian army closing in around the Men of Erin and making ready to strike. It was a nervous Queen that sat there with her men of war waiting to hear what Fergus was going to tell them.

'We hear strange tales of a youthful warrior of Ulster, who is famous for his warlike feats. Could it be that he is leading a band against us?' asked Ailell of Fergus, whom he seated at his right hand.

'No band of warriors has he but himself alone,' said Fergus. 'It is he and none other who is causing the havoc that the Men of Erin suffer to-day, for he is equal in strength, skill and daring to many men. When he was five years old Setanta had no equal among the youths of Conor's Boy-Corps at any of the games they were wont to play. At seven he took arms and slew three men on that day. Soon after that he went across the sea to Alba to study warfare with the woman warrior, Sgatha. To-day he is seventeen years old, and he must have the strength and skill of any ten men.'

'If Setanta was his name, why do others speak of him as Cuchullin, or the Hound of Culann?' asked Maeve.

'Setanta,' said Fergus, 'was his name until he was seven years old. Then, owing to a deed of warrior strength which he performed on the hound of Culann, the blacksmith to King Conor, he was named Cu Culann for ever after.

'It happened that King Conor, while on his way to an ale feast given in his honour by Culann, his smith, stopped to watch the Boy-Corps at a game of hurling. On this occasion young Setanta was playing alone against a team of twelve of the Boy-Corps. No ball passed Setanta's hurley as he stood in between his own goal-posts, but many were the balls that he sent home between the goal-posts of the Boy-Corps. As the King watched the game, so delighted was he with the good hurling of Setanta that he had the little boy called to him for special praise, and to honour him he bade him come to the banquet which Culann was preparing. Setanta thanked the King and promised to follow when the game would be over.'

Fergus then told how Conor went on to the house of

Culann, where he was seated in the place of honour by the smith, and all the warriors of the Red Branch were seated with him in order of their rank and age. This done, the smith, going to the King, asked if all his warriors had come, or if he expected any more to follow him to the banquet. The King told that all had indeed arrived, and in so saying quite forgot the invitation he had given to the small boy whose hurling had so pleased him.

'Then,' said the smith, 'I can untie my most excellent watch-dog and let him out to guard the bounds of my land. He has the strength and savage fury of a hundred ordinary dogs, and no ten men can get by him without being torn to pieces.'

'Let him loose by all means,' said Conor.

So Culann unleashed the dog, and gave orders for the food and wine to be put before his guests, and told his minstrels and men of poetry to begin their rhymes and tunes.

It was just then that the young Setanta, having won his game against the Boy-Corps, was coming over the fields, hitting his ball in front of him as he came. As the boy drew near the ramparts of Culann's fort, the fierce dog, hearing the sound of Setanta's hurley hitting the ball, set up a thunderous barking and growling, and with jaws wide open he rushed forward to tear him to pieces.

Inside in the banqueting hall the King and Culann's company, hearing the ferocious barking of the dog, stopped their talking and put down their wine-cups to listen. Then terror seized the King, for he knew that it must be the little Setanta that the bloodthirsty dog was tearing to pieces. Without a word he rushed from the hall and out on to the ramparts of Culann's fort, closely followed by all his warriors with their swords drawn to protect their King. There in the glare of a torch stood the boy with his hurley in his hand and the great hound lying dead and bleeding at his feet, for as the watch-dog had sprung on him, Setanta had seized him by the throat, and dashed his brains out against the pillar-stone of the gate.

Conor and his warriors gathered around the boy and with pride in his bravery they lifted him up to bear him into the banquet. But Setanta, looking back, seeing the smith standing over the body of his faithful dog and looking sadly down at it, called out to him:

'I will search all the land until I find another hound for you as good as this one you have just lost. Until then I myself will be your hound, and guard your house and lands.'

And so from that moment Conor christened him Cuchullin, or the hound of Culann, and that is the name he has been known by ever since.

'And so,' said Fergus, 'if as a lad of seven he could slay a dog whom not less than ten men would have faced alone, surely at the age of seventeen he can do as much harm as a company of warriors against Ulster's foes.'

Then Cormac, son of Conor, King of Ulster, who was in exile with Fergus, told Maeve and Ailell more of Cuchullin's youthful deeds of valour.

'The story of the day that Cuchullin took arms,' said Cormac, 'is the most wondrous story of all. It was the year after he got his name that Cuchullin sat listening to Caffa, the Druid, instructing his pupils, and as he told them of good omens and ill omens he said that certain days were lucky for some deeds and unlucky for others.

'"This day now," said Caffa, "would be a lucky day for a young man to take up arms for the first time. For anyone taking up arms to-day will be the greatest champion that ever was in Erin. His life will be fleeting, but the praise of his deeds will be in the mouths of all."'

Then Cormac went on to tell how Cuchullin, on hearing this, laid aside his hurley and ball, and going to the King asked that he should be given arms. The King, to please the lad, gave him two spears, a shield and a sword of the kind he kept for his Boy-Corps, to teach them the use of arms.

Cuchullin took the weapons and began to flourish and bend them to try their strength, but one after the other they splintered in his hand. Seeing this, the King gave stronger weapons to the boy, but again, he broke them as easily as he would a rotten stick.

'These, O King, are but the weapons of a common warrior,' said Cuchullin, 'and they suit not me.'

The King then gave Cuchullin weapons that were specially tempered and made for himself, and these Cuchullin could not break.

'Take them,' said the King, 'and may they bring thee glory and renown.'

Cuchullin then got into Conor's chariot, and bade the charioteer drive him to the border in search of deeds of valour. At the border Cuchullin had the charioteer drive him up to the top of the highest hill he could see, in order to view the country. From there the charioteer pointed out to him the forts and duns of the most important chiefs living there, and the last one he showed him was the fort of the three fierce sons of Nechtan the Mighty.

'It is said of the sons of Nechtan,' said the charioteer, 'that the Ulstermen who are alive are not as many as the Ulstermen who have fallen by the hands of the three of them.'

'I will this day challenge the sons of Nechtan,' said Cuchullin, and he leaped into the chariot, bidding the charioteer to drive him to their fort.

'Only a foolhardy warrior would go to Nechtan's fort,' said the charioteer.

'I will go nevertheless,' said Cuchullin, and ordered the charioteer to make haste.

Reaching the fort of the three fierce brothers, Cuchullin jumped out of the chariot and struck a loud resounding blow on the pole of combat. Then Foill, the eldest, came rushing out of the dun. When he saw such a young lad as Cuchullin before him he made to turn back into the dun, but Cuchullin bade him get his weapons and challenged him to combat.

When Foill came back armed for combat Cuchullin took a ball of tempered iron, and, putting it in his sling, he cast it at him. Before Foill could strike one blow the iron ball entered his forehead, went clean through his skull, and the first of the fierce sons of Nechtan fell dead. Cuchullin then took his head and bound it to his chariot-rim. Then each in his turn the other two brothers came out and attacked Cuchullin, but these he also slew and bound their heads to his chariot-rim.

Cuchullin then got into his chariot and set out in triumph back to Emain Macha to present King Conor with the heads of his three bitterest enemies.

'And now, O Queen,' said Cormac to Maeve, 'if these deeds were done by a boy not yet seven years old, it is not to be wondered at that his deeds as a fully grown warrior should go far towards hindering your army.'

'It is true indeed,' said Maeve, and she called Fergus to her and asked him to go to Cuchullin and arrange a parley between them on the morrow.

III

# *Cuchullin Parleys with Maeve*

THE night after Fergus had told her of the youthful deeds of valour that had made Cuchullin famous as a champion, Maeve sat apart in her tent pondering on all she had heard, and trying to make up her mind how she would deal with this opponent who was stopping her path into Ulster, and killing so many of her warriors. She was curious, too, to see the youthful warrior with her own eyes. So she decided to parley with him herself, and not to send Fergus, for Fergus spoke with too much praise of Cuchullin, with too much love and affection for him, and with too much pride in his warlike skill.

There and then she called her messengers to her, and in the dark of the winter's night she sent them out to creep secretly through the encampment and seek out Cuchullin in his hillside bothy.

Cuchullin heard the messengers and sent back word to Maeve that he would meet her in parley in a nearby glen after sunrise.

One hour after sunrise Maeve, accompanied by Ailell, went to the glen, and seeing Cuchullin already there before them, they went to the hill on the opposite side from where he was so as to keep the glen between them during the parley. Then the talks began, and her runners sped to and fro between them with Maeve's offers and Cuchullin's answers to her. Maeve started by sending to Cuchullin many flattering messages and compliments; then she offered him great tracts of land in Connacht and her own friendship for ever if he would forsake the cause of Ulster and King Conor and come over to her side and the Men of Erin.

These terms Cuchullin refused, sent back her runner and left the glen. Almost at once he started to harass her troops more than ever.

All night long he moved quickly around the edge of the encampment picking off men singly and in groups, and all through the night stones from his sling whistled over their heads, so that no one in that vast camp was safe, and no sleep was got by anyone, least of all by Maeve. And as they marched on by day into Ulster, Cuchullin was on the path before them, and though nobody could catch sight of him, he continued to cut off their men in twos and threes, so that in the end it was reckoned that one hundred of the Men of Erin fell by Cuchullin's hand each day.

One evening while the men were making camp Maeve stood with some of her women in the middle of the encampment, taking the air. On one shoulder Maeve had her little pet bird, and her pet squirrel sat on the other. They spoke in whispers of Cuchullin's latest exploits against them, Maeve telling of how that day he had fallen on a troop of her men as they were cutting a path through a wood, and how he had killed all save one who had come back with the tale. In the middle of the story a sharp whistling sound was heard overhead, and as Maeve looked around, to see from whence it had come, her pet bird fell dead at her feet. Terrified, Maeve now made for her tent as quickly as she could run, but before she reached it another stone from Cuchullin's sling hit her squirrel and knocked him off her shoulder dead on the ground before her as she ran.

Reaching her tent, Maeve sent for Fergus and asked him to go at once to Cuchullin and ask him what terms he would accept.

When Cuchullin saw Fergus draw near he went out to meet him. The two friends embraced each other, and Cuchullin welcomed Fergus with joy and delight.

'Welcome, Fergus, my childhood's friend, my foster-father and guardian,' said Cuchullin, and he led him into his shelter and bade Laegh, his charioteer, put food and ale before them.

Then Fergus told Cuchullin of the business that he had with him and begged him to pardon him if his visit seemed short. 'For,' said Fergus, 'I dare not stay to talk to thee at this time, O my beloved foster-son, for the Men of Erin doubt me, and will think if I overstay my time that I am proving traitor to their cause and betraying them to thee. But one thing I ask thee in all love and affection—that if at any time we find ourselves against each other in battle, face to face, thou for love of me will turn and run before my blade, for never could I be forced to redden it on my foster-son and pupil. Promise, O Cuchullin.'

'I am indeed thy foster-son and thy friend,' said Cuchullin, 'and dearly do I love thee, but never have I turned my back on my foes, and loath am I to promise. Rather would I grant thee any other thing than this.'

'Do this thing that I ask thee,' said Fergus, 'and in the grand and final battle of the Raid, when Conor's hosts will have thrown off their pains, then will I flee from thee, and so your honour will at last be saved.'

'And I will gain a stroke for Ulster,' said Cuchullin. 'I do agree, and willingly give my word.'

Then they spoke of Maeve's message to Cuchullin, and Fergus asked him what terms he would accept to stop the constant harassing of Maeve's army and permit them to sleep peacefully in the camp at night. Cuchullin said that Maeve should not advance into Ulster by forced marches, but that she should send a champion to engage Cuchullin in single combat each day, and that while the combat went on her army could advance, but once her champion was slain they should halt until next day.

Fergus then took leave of Cuchullin and brought his terms back to Maeve, who, on hearing them, said:

'It is better that one man should be slain each day than that a hundred should fall at night, even though that one man be a champion.'

At first Maeve kept to these conditions and sent a champion each day to the ford to fight with Cuchullin in single combat, her armies advancing while her champion stood up. But so short was the time that even the best of her champions lasted before being slain by Cuchullin that it was but little progress that the Men of Erin made. So that her army should not be halted too soon, she began to send one champion after another to keep Cuchullin engaged, and he got no respite from sunrise till the coming of darkness. Then, seeing the number of her champions that Cuchullin was slaying, she broke all the conditions of the agreement and sent one hundred warriors against him all at once.

In a desperate struggle he fought against the hundred and held the ford against them. In twos and threes at a time he slew them, leaving their bodies in heaps around him in the river, so that the place was called 'Ath Cro', or 'the ford of the slaughter' from that day to this.

Weary and sorely wounded, Cuchullin rested that night standing leaning on his spear on a hillock overlooking the camp of the Men of Erin. His charioteer, Laegh, kindled a fire and bade him take what rest he could, for since the Raid began, three months before, Cuchullin knew no rest night nor day, only for such short naps as he might snatch leaning against his spear, his head on his fist, his fist clasping his spear, and his spear resting on his knee.

In such a position Cuchullin now stood by Laegh's fire and looked down on the camp of the Men of Erin. As he looked, he saw the glinting and gleaming of a thousand burnished weapons shining in the camp-fires of the vast camp that stretched far and wide over the great plain of Ulster. At the sight a sudden anger seized him, and grasping his two javelins, his shield and his sword all at once, he brandished his sword, beat on his shield till it rang with a deafening din, and whirled his spear. Then, opening his mouth to its widest, he gave forth his 'hero call'. So blood-curdling was the cry that the demons of the air, the goblins, elves and other sprites of the glen answered it, and filled the air with horrible sound. Maddened by fear, the Men of Erin jumped up in confusion, and in the dark grasped their weapons, ran on each other's spear-points in panic, and thrust at each other blindly, so that from panic and terror alone in the heart of the camp one hundred warriors died. That night was ever after spoken of as 'The Great Carnage'.

Secretly now Maeve led off a third of her army northwards to seek the bull. Cuchullin followed her and harassed her rear for many miles, but he had to turn back to defend Muirthemne, his own country, from the main body of the Men of Erin. Maeve and her company found the bull in a valley near Slieve Gullion and drove him and his fifteen heifers south to put him in hiding behind the camp of the Men of Erin. Cuchullin came on them and challenged the leading herdsman to single combat to recover the bull. But while the combat was on, the other drovers drove off the bull to the camp of the Men of Erin. Losing the Brown Bull on this occasion by the deception and trickery of the herdsmen was the greatest affront and treachery that Cuchullin endured in the whole course of the war. That night he returned to his shelter on the hillside overlooking the Men of Erin, and he was weary, sorely wounded and sad at heart for having suffered the Brown Bull of Ulster to slip past him into the territory of Ulster's enemies.

As Cuchullin rested on his spear, Laegh looked out over the enemy's camp, and he saw a lone warrior come towards them from the north-east, cross through the encampment without hindrance, and make in a straight line towards where he and Cuchullin stood.

'A man of strange and noble bearing comes towards us, little Cu,' said Laegh.

'What figure of a man is he?' asked Cuchullin.

'A tall and comely man walking proudly as a god,' answered Laegh. 'He is wearing a green mantle fastened at his throat with a silver brooch. Next his skin he wears a

tunic of royal silk embroidered with red gold. He carries a black shield with a rim of white bronze, and in his hand he has a five-barbed spear and a pronged javelin. He walks through the great camp as if none can see him, for no man notices him and he heeds no one.'

'It is in truth one of my fairy kin coming to solace me,' said Cuchullin.

It was indeed Lugh of the Long Arm, the sun god and mystical father of Cuchullin, and he had come to soothe the champion's wounds with healing balm, and to bid him rest. Drawing close he spoke to Cuchullin:

'Sleep thou a little while now, O Cuchullin, and in thy sleep I will heal your wounds.'

Then he sang over him a sweet and soothing tune, and Cuchullin fell into a heavy sleep. For three days Cuchullin slept, and the warrior from Faery laid healing herbs and oils on his cuts and gaping wounds, so that while he slept his wounds and gashes were healed and he was brought back to his full vigour.

At the end of three days Cuchullin awoke, and, shaking off his sleep, he sat up and looked at Lugh, who had been keeping watch over him. He asked him how long he had lain there in slumber and if the Men of Erin had been allowed to go on into Ulster without anyone attacking them during his sleep.

Lugh answered that he had been for three days asleep, and during that time the Ulster Boy-Corps had marched down from the north and had three times given battle to Maeve's army, killing three times their own number of the Men of Erin.

Cuchullin then asked how fared the Boy-Corps in that struggle.

'Alas,' answered Lugh, 'though they hewed down three times their own number of the Men of Erin the Boy-Corps now is no more.'

'Thrice alas that I was not there in my strength,' said Cuchullin, and he called on Laegh to tackle for him his scythed chariot, for he was going out to avenge the destruction of the Boy-Corps.

Laegh then tackled the horses under the armoured chariot and threw over them the iron sheet and the gold-embroidered coats of mail that covered them from forehead to forehand. Then he mounted the chariot that was studded with darts and lances and spears so that it bristled with sharp spikes like a giant hedgehog, and he cast a spell of invisibility over himself and his horses.

Cuchullin then arose and arrayed himself in a special war dress, seized his weapons, and with Laegh drove off to the camp of the Men of Erin.

At first he had Laegh drive in a wide circle around the enemy camp, and then he had him drive through their ranks, and as he went he mowed them down like ripe corn, leaving their bodies in long swathes on either side of the chariot's way. Three times he circled in and around his foes in this manner, and three times more he went back again, killing hound and horse and man, and leaving them in great piles behind him. For they were all one to Cuchullin that night in the Great Rout on the Plain of Muirthemne when he avenged the youths of Ulster on the men of the four provinces of Erin.

IV

# *The Fight with Ferdia*

In Maeve's army at this time there was one champion who was equal to Cuchullin in bravery and in warlike skill. This was Ferdia, son of Damon. These two heroes had long been friends and companions, for together they had learned the art of warlike feats from Sgatha, the woman warrior in the Isle of Skye. There they had grown up to manhood, from there they had gone side by side through many adventures in far countries—they had sealed their love and friendship in blood in many a dangerous fight.

Now, Ferdia was a man of Connacht, and when Maeve sent out her call to arms for the fight against Ulster, Ferdia had come with all his fighting men to join her army. But when he came with the Men of Erin to the Gap of the North and found that his boyhood comrade, Cuchullin, stood alone defending his country against the whole army of Maeve, Ferdia resolved to take no part in such an unfair fight. So he kept to his own bothy, which he told his men to pitch for him every night on the edge of the encampment, as far as possible from the quarters of Queen Maeve and King Ailell. He hoped that by keeping out of her eye

Maeve would not call on him to go against Cuchullin in single combat. Each day, too, he used to send secret messengers to watch Cuchullin fight the champions that Maeve sent against him, hoping that no harm would come to him, and that he might even be able to help him if the struggle proved too hard. Every evening when his messengers came back with tidings of Cuchullin's victories and bravery, Ferdia was glad for his old comrade.

As the fighting went on and Cuchullin kept slaying one champion after another, Maeve began to find it hard to persuade her warriors to stand up against him, until at last a day came when she had to call a council of her wise men and captains of war to ask whether there was no man in her army could match Cuchullin.

'Why,' said her chief men, and they were all on the one word, 'do you not send Ferdia, son of Damon?'

And with one voice they assured her that for bravery and deeds of valour Ferdia was the equal of Cuchullin.

'In one school they were trained, and it is known that in skill and knowledge they are one in all things.'

'It is a good choice,' said Maeve. 'Ferdia shall go.'

She called for a runner there and then, and bade him go to the tent of Ferdia and tell him that she and Ailell would have him attend them in their royal quarters.

When he saw Maeve's runner before his tent Ferdia knew that what he feared most was about to happen; he sent the messenger back to Maeve. Maeve thereupon ordered her druids and men of poetry to make mocking rhymes, and to sing them before Ferdia, to revile and disgrace him in front of his followers and all the Men of Erin so that they would hold him in contempt for the rest of his life. When Ferdia heard these satires being sung outside his tent a great shame came over him, and he decided to go to the quarters of Ailell and Maeve.

Maeve, seeing him come on, came forward herself and received him with all the honour due to a great champion. She called together her captains and chief men and ordered that a banquet should be held in his honour, and when the royal company sat at table she placed Ferdia at her own right hand. Then she placed Finnebar, her daughter, at Ferdia's side, and bade her see to it that she kept the hero's goblet full, and to fill it with her own hand of the choicest wines only. When the wine-cup had been filled many times Maeve began to flatter Ferdia and to speak of his great deeds of bravery that were known to everyone of the eastern and western world. Then she offered him large rewards—grants of land, her own friendship for ever, and her daughter, Finnebar, in marriage if he would go against the destroyer of her hosts—Cuchullin.

When the assembly heard Maeve's offer of rewards they exclaimed aloud at their generosity, except Ferdia, who kept silent. All turned towards him to hear his answer to the Queen's offer, and as he stood up Finnebar filled his goblet once more and, kissing it, handed it up to him with a smile. Ferdia stood, confused with all this praise and generosity and feasting in his honour, and troubled in his mind too, for the memory of his love for Cuchullin and of their youth in shadow-land came back to him. So, looking at Maeve, who with her chief men eagerly awaited his answer, he said:

'Thy gifts truly are great and generous, O Maeve, but I will leave them and never accept them if their price be to do battle with my foster-brother, that man of my love and of my affection, Cuchullin.' And then Ferdia spoke a lay telling of the bonds between them—

'We were heart companions once,
We were comrades in the woods,
We were men that shared a bed,
When we slept the weary sleep,
After hard and bitter fights. . . .'

Maeve now saw that a bond of love and esteem such as that between Ferdia and Cuchullin could not be broken either by flattery or bribes. She therefore thought of another plan, and when Ferdia had finished his lay telling of all the perilous adventures that he and Cuchullin had shared, and which bound them in blood to one another, she pretended she had not heard a single word he had spoken. Turning aside to some of her chief men, she said very quietly:

'It seems to me now quite true what Cuchullin has said of Ferdia.'

'What has Cuchullin said of me?' demanded Ferdia.

'He said that you are wise not to go against him in single combat,' answered Maeve.

Ferdia now burst out in anger at this, saying:

'It was not just of Cuchullin to speak so of me. He cannot truly say that he has ever seen either cowardice or lack of boldness in me in all our time together. I swear by my arms of valour that I shall be the first to offer him combat by to-morrow's dawn, loath though I am to do it.'

Then in silence and gloom Ferdia sought his own quarters. That night there was no sound of music or song from Ferdia's followers, and no one spoke above a whisper, as with anxious glances they watched their master come back from Maeve's feasting. They knew that brave and skilful as their master was, Cuchullin was just as skilful and just as brave. They knew, too, that when two such champions would meet in combat one of them must be slain.

Ferdia rested till dawn, and then called for his chariot to be yoked so that he should go early to the ford and be there before Cuchullin. His charioteer got the horses, yoked them to the chariot and then, going to Ferdia, tried to persuade him not to go against Cuchullin. But Ferdia told him that he had no wish to fight his foster-brother, but that since he had given his word to Ailell and Maeve he was determined to keep it. Then, overcome with grief and anger at the thing he was compelled to do, he turned around to the camp of the Men of Erin and, raising his voice, he shouted aloud:

'By my conscience I had almost liefer fall by Cuchullin's hand than that he should fall by mine. And should Cuchullin fall by my hand to-day, then shall Maeve and many of the Men of Erin fall by my hand too, because of the pledge they extorted from me and I drunken and merry.'

Then he stepped into his chariot and drove to the ford of combat. On reaching the ford he bade his charioteer lay out the chariot poles over his head and lay the skin coverings over them. Then he put cushions and rugs on the ground so that he might sleep there till Cuchullin should come.

While Ferdia lay asleep at the ford Fergus left the camp of the Men of Erin and went to Cuchullin to warn him that it was Ferdia, his friend and his equal in all warlike feats, that was to meet him in combat on the following day.

'As my soul liveth,' said Cuchullin, when he heard this, 'it is not such an encounter as I would wish with my friend, not out of fear but out of love and affection for him. I would almost prefer to fall by the hand of that warrior than that he should fall by mine.'

Cuchullin then lay down to rest, and he did not rise early that day, for fear that the Men of Erin would say that he had awakened early through fear of Ferdia. The sun was high in the sky when he stepped into his chariot to go to the ford. As he reached the ford Ferdia stood waiting for him on the southern side of the river. When Cuchullin got down from his chariot Ferdia bade him welcome.

'Ah, Ferdia,' said Cuchullin sadly, 'truly spoken was thy welcome for me up to this. But to-day I put no more trust in it, since you have given up our friendship for the sake of the false promises of a treacherous woman.'

Sorely hurt at hearing Cuchullin upbraid him, Ferdia called out: 'Too long have we spent already in exchange of words, rather let our weapons speak for us now.'

So, going towards one another, they began to cast their small spears, and backwards and forwards they plied between them, like bees with the sun on their wings on a fine summer's day. So they fought all day, changing their weapons from time to time, and so evenly matched was their skill in attack and in defence that not one of their many weapons was reddened when at nightfall they agreed to stop the combat for that day.

Then, throwing their weapons behind them to their charioteers, the two champions went towards each other, and each putting his arms around the neck of the other, kissed with brotherly affection three times.

Then their charioteers made up a litter of fresh rushes for each of them, with pillows for their heads. And special messengers came with healing herbs and cures from the fairy dwellings of Erin and laid them on Cuchullin's aching limbs. And of every herb and potion he got Cuchullin sent a share across the ford to Ferdia.

And the Men of Erin brought food and drink of every kind to Ferdia, and of each food and drink he got, Ferdia sent a portion north across the ford to Cuchullin.

That night their horses were in the same paddock and their two charioteers sat at the same fire.

Next day at sunrise they took up the fight once more. This time they fought from their chariots with their broad spears. All day they struck and received many a strong blow until night came and they agreed again to stop. By this time so gashed and torn was each of their bodies that it is said that the birds of the air could fly in and out through their wounds.

When they stopped fighting, as on the first night, they threw aside their weapons and embraced each other in the middle of the ford. That night, too, they sent each other food and medicine, and their horses were put in the one paddock and their charioteers shared the same fire.

Next morning when they met to start the fight once more Cuchullin saw at the first glance that a change had come over Ferdia. There was a gloomy look on his face, and he no longer seemed able to hold himself upright, and when he walked his steps were slow and dragging. Seeing this, a great sadness seized Cuchullin. Eagerly he went across the ford towards Ferdia, and again reminding him of their one-time friendship and love for each other he begged him to give up the struggle. But Ferdia hung his head, so as not to look at Cuchullin, and answered sadly that he could not now break his pledge with Maeve. So there and then they settled what weapons they would use that day and took up the fight again. All day long, in mournful silence, they continued to thrust and to parry, to hew and to hack, until at evening's close they gave up for the night.

Sadly and silently they cast aside their weapons, and each, without a word to the other, sought his own side of the ford. This time their parting was mournful indeed, without a word of goodwill or farewell between them. That night their horses were not put in the same paddock, and each charioteer sat at his own fire. No word or message passed between them during the long night.

Early next morning Ferdia rose and put on his battle suit, which, with its many coverings of thick hide and an apron of iron, was intended to protect his body from the dreaded barbed spear, the Gae Bulga, Cuchullin's most famous weapon. Then Cuchullin appeared and the fight began. All day long they struggled fiercely. So strong were the blows they gave that the shield of each was buckled from rim to centre. The noise was so great that the very demons of the air cried out and shrieked with terror over their heads. So furious was their trampling that the river was put out of its course, and not a drop of water remained in its bed under their feet.

Towards evening, taking Cuchullin in an unguarded moment, Ferdia managed to press home his sword up to the very hilt in that hero's body so that his blood ran like a stream across the ford. Before he could recover Ferdia passed his sword twice more in quick heavy strokes through his chest.

It was then that Cuchullin called to Laegh for the Gae Bulga. Taking careful aim, he cast it, sending it through the iron apron, and all Ferdia's coverings and protective armour until it dug its deadly barbs deep into his flesh.

'The end has come now at last, O Cuchullin,' said Ferdia, and he dropped to the ground.

Seeing Ferdia fall, Cuchullin threw down his arms and ran towards him. He bent over him and taking him in his arms tenderly and sadly he carried him across the ford, so that he should lie on the north side with himself, and not on the south with the Men of Erin. There Cuchullin sank down beside his friend and began to mourn deeply over him. Sunken in grief and forgetful of all danger, Cuchullin remained weeping over Ferdia his comrade until Laegh,

his charioteer, counselled him to leave the ford before the Men of Erin should come in their numbers and attack him. Then, slowly raising his head, he looked up at Laegh and in a sad, gentle voice said:

'O my friend Laegh, know that every other combat and fight I took on was but a game and a play compared with this fight with Ferdia.'

Then Cuchullin spoke a lay over his dead friend.

'Play was each, pleasure each,
    Till Ferdia faced the beach;
One had been our student life,
    One in strife of school our place,
One our gentle teacher's grace,
    Loved o'er all and each.

Play was each, pleasure each,
    Till Ferdia faced the beach;
One had been our wonted ways,
    One the praise for feat of fields,
Sgatha gave two victor shields
    Equal prize to each.

Play was each, pleasure each,
    Till Ferdia faced the beach;
Dear that pillar of pure gold
    Who fell cold beside the ford
Hosts of heroes felt his sword
    First in battle-breach.

Play was each, pleasure each,
    Till Ferdia faced the beach;
Lion fiery, fierce and bright,
    Wave whose might no thing withstands,
Sweeping, with the shrinking sands,
    Horror o'er the beach.

Play was each, pleasure each,
    Till Ferdia faced the beach;
Loved Ferdia, dear to me;
    I shall dree his death for aye,
Yesterday a mountain he—
    But a shade to-day.'

V

# *Ulster Awake*

AFTER the combat with Ferdia, Cuchullin lay in his shelter sorely wounded, weak in body and spirit. His strength had left him, and he knew he was no longer able to keep the Men of Erin from over-running Ulster. Now, Cuchullin's father, Sualtach, heard of the sad condition of his son and came south to help him. When he saw Cuchullin covered with wounds and bloody bruises, Sualtach began to weep and lament over him, but Cuchullin bade him cease lamenting and to go at once to King Conor and bid him come with his warriors to drive the Men of Erin from their lands, for he was no longer able to keep them back single-handed.

'All alone am I,' he said, 'against the four provinces of Erin, every day slaying a man at a ford and one hundred warriors at night. Fair fight is not granted to me nor single combat, and no one comes to aid or succour me. Twigs hold my mantle over me and dried sops of grass are stuffed into my wounds.'

Sualtach then, at his son's bidding, took one of the chariot horses, the Grey of Macha, and set out for the royal palace of Conor at Emain, to take the news to Ulster and to arouse her warriors.

When he reached Emain Macha he rode around the outer ramparts of the royal dun shouting his call to arms:

'In Ulster men are being slain, women carried off and kine driven. Arise, ye men of Ulster, and save your lands.'

Three times he rode around the ramparts shouting his warning, but not a sound of living person from the royal palace was there to answer his call, and the Hall of the Red Branch Knights was as silent as a ruin. No warrior kept a look-out from the ramparts and no sentinel guarded the door of the palace. Inside the fort the warriors lay huddled in deep sleep, some on the floor and some still sitting at the festive board, while around them lay their weapons, dull and rusty from want of use. Sualtach rode through the halls and corridors still shouting his warning, but no warrior moved except to groan as if in pain. The only answer he got to his shouting was the hollow echo from the rafters.

In fury, when he could get no one to heed him, Sualtach turned his horse about quickly, thinking to go back to Cuchullin. But in his impatience he dragged the bridle-rein too roughly and the Grey of Macha reared up furiously, stumbled over a sleeping warrior and threw Sualtach forward on its neck. Sualtach's head struck sharply against the rim of his shield and was cut clean off his body. The head fell to the ground, while the lifeless body still lay across the horse's neck, and from where it lay in the dust the head still kept on warning the King and warriors of Ulster:

'Your women are being slain, your cattle driven off and your houses are being burnt by the Men of Erin. Arise, ye men of Ulster, and drive them from your lands.'

After many hours the constant shouting of the head at last pierced the nightmare slumber of the King, and opening his eyes he looked at it.

'That head is too noisy, put it on the pillar of the room so that it may rest,' he mumbled, and sank back into deep slumber once more.

A warrior lying near the King, hearing the royal command, rose to do his bidding, and placed the head on the top of a pillar in the centre of the room, and he, too, fell back into slumber once again.

But now from the top of the pillar louder and louder grew the shouting of the head, till at last one warrior rose on his elbow and listened. And as he listened to its frenzied shouting, he saw the headless body of Sualtach astride the horse that, terrified, was standing stock still in the middle of the room, and he broke into loud savage laughter. As he laughed, the head shouted louder than ever, until the palace was filled with wild and barbarous sound.

The King now awoke, and hearing the head he jumped to his feet and swore a mighty oath:

'Unless the heavens with their showers of stars fall to the ground, unless the furrowed, blue-bordered ocean break over the rocky brow of the earth, I will restore every cow to her byre and every woman to her hearth.'

Then, waking the warriors around him, he called for his captains of war and ordered his runners to be sent out in all directions to rally the men of Ulster, and to bid them to muster their hosts and get ready to march southwards against the Men of Erin.

When the scouts of Maeve brought word to her that the Ultonians were getting ready for the war against her armies, she sent out Mac Roth, the Herald, to scan the great plain of Meath for any signs of the Ulster army marching against her, and if there was she bade him find out in what numbers they came.

As Mac Roth watched the Plain of Meath he saw a heavy, grey mist fill the glens and the valleys, and rise like a shroud into the upper air, veiling the space between the earth and the heavens. It seemed to him that the hills were islands in a lake that rose up out of the valleys of mist. Then he saw wide, yawning caverns leading into the mist, and showers of white snowflakes falling through it. He saw what he thought was a flock of black-and-white birds flying and wheeling in and around the misty caverns, and a sparkling of shining stars glinting and glistening as on a night of hoar-frost. Then he heard a multitude of tumultuous noises like the rushing of a hundred mountain torrents, the rumbling of thunder between high hills, the pounding of a mighty sea on a shingly beach and the roaring and rushing of a great wind.

Back went Mac Roth to Maeve with these tidings, and greatly wondering at what they might portend, she sent for Fergus Mac Roy.

'The great grey mist filling the glens and hollows,' said Fergus, 'was the streaming breaths of the horses and men of Conor's army who are hastening southward to drive the Men of Erin out of Ulster.

'And the islands in the lakes were the heads of the heroes over their horses' breath.

'And the wide yawning caverns leading into the mist were the mouths and nostrils of the horses wide-open and inhaling and exhaling the wind quickly with the great speed of their coming.

'And the flock of birds that Mac Roth saw,' said Fergus, 'were but the clods of earth and sods, flung up by the hooves of the galloping horses hurrying to the destruction of the Men of Erin.'

'And the snowflakes of which he talks ?' asked Ailell.

'They were the foam and froth that the bridles flung from the bits of their strong steeds.

'And the stars shining and sparkling through the mist as in the heavens on a frosty night were the eyes of the warriors of Ulster blazing with fury and rage as they hasten to redden their swords in the blood of their enemies.

'And the tumult of noise,' said Fergus, 'was the crashing of shields, the jangle of javelins, the ringing of helmets and the clangour of breastplates, the straining of ropes, the whirr of wheels, the tramping of horses and the creaking of chariots, and the great battle-cry of the fierce and terrible, bloodthirsty Warriors of the Red Branch hastening to the cleaving and the carving, the hewing and the hacking of the Men of Erin.'

'We make not much of all this,' answered Maeve with great calm. 'We await them with our good warriors and champion fighting men.'

'Thou shalt have need of them,' said Fergus, 'for neither in Erin nor in Alba is there any force that can quell Ulster once their fury is kindled.'

Then, hearing that the armies of Ulster were collecting on the Hill of Slane in Meath, Maeve sent out Mac Roth once more to bring her back word of their numbers.

The herald soon returned with the account of a huge host pouring in from Ulster and taking up their position on the Hill of Slane.

'From early morning's first dim glimmering till the evening twilight, the earth,' he told her, 'was not naked once under them.'

He told of many corps of warriors, each under its own leader and with its own coloured battle costume. He told of corps of druids, who while marching along kept raising their eyes to heaven, watching the clouds and crying out their spells to set the elements at war over the heads of their enemies.

He told of a corps of leeches under the leadership of Finghin the Leech in which each man was dressed in a special garb and carried at his waist a small bag containing his medicines and surgical instruments. Finghin was known to Maeve as a clever and learned doctor, for it was said that Finghin need only see the smoke from a sick man's chimney for him to say from what disease he was suffering.

Then he told of a company with heavy armour such as castles on wheels, and weapons known as 'battle wheels'. The wheels, Mac Roth told them, were rolled into the enemy ranks, causing them to break and run in disorder.

Now, all this time, while their herald told Maeve and Ailell of the hosts of Ulster that were gathering on the Hill of Slane, Cuchullin lay on his bed, to which Laegh and some of the Men of Ulster had bound him with ropes to keep him out of the fighting until his wounds should heal. Hearing from Laegh of the coming of the Ulstermen,

Cuchullin bade him go with messages from him to stir them up against the Men of Erin to their greatest fury. Laegh did as Cuchullin ordered, and so well did he rouse them, telling them of Cuchullin's lone stand for Ulster and of Maeve's treachery to him, that many of them jumped up still naked and seized their weapons to make immediate battle with Maeve's army. And it is said that those of them whose tent doors faced eastwards forced a way out through the tent westwards, not taking the time to go around by the door. Just then Conor's druids and Men of Magic proclaimed that Ulster's lucky time had come, the sun being fully risen and flooding the valleys and glens with its bright yellow light. So, with a great brandishing of weapons and blood-curdling whoops of war the Men of Ulster went into battle against the Men of Erin.

Maeve now called for her chariot, and with her weapons in her hand, her golden circlet on her head and her honey-coloured hair flowing behind her, the great Queen rode proudly out at the head of her army to meet the Ultonians.

Fergus, Ailell and Maeve went together into the thick of the battle, to spur on the men of Erin and to direct the attack. Three times they drove back the Men of Ulster, but each time the Ulstermen recovered, and in the end they held their own against Maeve and Ailell, who led a ferocious attack against them.

Conor now took the field to see for himself why his men were being driven back, and in the fighting he came face to face with Fergus, his bitterest enemy, whose kingdom he had taken, and of whose exile he had been the cause by his treachery to the Sons of Usnach. Fergus stood in front of his old enemy, and he struck three resounding blows on Conor's shield. Now, as Conor's shield always cried out when its owner was in danger, men rushed from all sides to protect their King. But Fergus lifted his sword again, this time with both hands, and prepared to strike a mighty blow. And mighty indeed it would be, for the sword of Fergus was one he had got from the Faery, and when raised to strike a blow it grew as long as a rainbow, and it was said of it that it never made two halves of any blow it struck. Now, Conor's son, Cormac, who had gone into exile with Fergus and was fighting that day with the Men of Erin, saw Fergus lift his sword to strike his father, held his arms from behind and begged him not to deliver the blow, but to turn sideways and to strike instead at the three hills that stood to their left. Fergus then turned aside from Conor, and with one swift blow of his sword sliced the heads off of three hillocks, and ever since the hills are known as ' The Three Topless Ones of Meath '.

Now, Cuchullin, having heard Conor's shield cry out, writhed in frenzy on his bed as he tried to break loose from the bindings that Laegh and the Ultonians had put on him. Then he gave a sudden spring, burst the bindings and sent them flying through the air till they landed seventy miles away in Connacht. His bracings flew off and landed in Corcumraud in Clare and the splints landed up in Ulster. Then his wounds opened and began to bleed again.

Rising from his bed, he looked for his weapons to go to the aid of Conor, but none of his arms could he find. Seizing the remnants of his chariot, that had been broken and battered in the fight with Ferdia, he threw it over his shoulder and went out to fight the Men of Erin.

He made for the thick of the battle, smiting any that came in his way as he went through the struggling, heaving throng, and as he went he called aloud for Fergus Mac Roy to come and face him.

' Come and face me, Fergus,' he shouted, ' or I swear if you do not I will grind thee as a mill grinds fresh grain, I will wash thee as a cup is washed in a tub, I will bind thee as the woodbine binds a tree, I will pounce on thee as a hawk pounces on fledglings, I will go over thee as a tail goes over a cat, and I will pound thee as the waves pound a fish on the strand.'

Fergus turned and asked who it was that dared to speak to him with such high-sounding words.

' It is I, O Fergus,' said Cuchullin, and then he reminded him of their agreement not to fight against one another:

'Thou didst promise to fly before me what time I should be wounded and in pools of gore and riddled in the battle of the Tain. For when thou hadst not thy sword with thee I did flee before thee.'

Fergus kept his pledge, for, turning around, he made a pretence of fleeing from Cuchullin, and as he fell back three thousand of the Leinstermen, which was Fergus' company, fell back with him. Seeing them withdraw the Munstermen drew back with them, and then all the Men of Erin broke their ranks and fled westward over the hill. Only the company of Ailell and Maeve held their ground. It was midday when Cuchullin first went into the battle, and by the time the pale sun of winter was following the Connacht men west behind the hill, the last company of Maeve's army had fled before him and the Ultonians.

Now, Maeve with a chosen company of her best warriors brought up the rear, and fought a number of rear-guard actions until such time as news was brought to her that the Brown Bull of Cooley, which she had sent on ahead, was safely across the Shannon in Connacht.

Cuchullin stood on the Leinster side of the mighty River Shannon watching the last stragglers of Maeve's retreating army, and his eye rested on three hilltops on the Connacht side of the river. Calling to Laegh to bring him his famous sword, 'The Hard-headed Steeling', he raised it till its tip touched the ground behind him, and with all his strength gave one mighty blow and cut the heads off of the three hills, and from that day they have been known as 'The Maolain' of Athlone, or 'The Flat Tops' of Athlone. So from that on whenever a man from the west should reproachfully speak of 'The Three Bald Tops of Meath' the man of Ulster could answer with 'The Three Topless Ones of Athlone'.

VI

# *The Battle of the Bulls*

THE night before the great rout of the Men of Erin by Conor and his Ulstermen Maeve sent the Brown Bull into Connacht for safety. In the dark middle of the night, chosen drovers and a small company of warriors secretly started out, and by little-known tracks and hidden ways drove the bull and his fifteen heifers west. At first light they had crossed the Shannon, and as the sun rose in the sky and the Brown Bull of Cooley saw the wild trackless country out in front of him, he threw back his head and, either with joy at its beauty, or with excitement at its strangeness, he let out a bellow that rolled like thunder from one end of Connacht to the other.

The White-Horned Bull of Ailell, hearing the bellow, stopped his grazing and lifted his head to listen, for up to now no other bull in Connacht dared to give out a sound that was any louder than the quiet, drowsy 'moo' of a milch cow that would be nuzzling her calf. The Brown Bull bellowed once more. The White-Horned tore up the sods under him, tossed his head angrily, and made off at a gallop for Royal Cruachan to find out what bull or cow dared to raise his voice so loud.

When the men of Maeve's household saw the bull appear on the ramparts, snorting and pawing the ground, they knew he was ready to fight the Brown, so they named Briciu as judge in the fight between them. Briciu was famous for his quarrels and as one always ready to stir up strife between others, his motto being ' strife is better than loneliness '. It was said of him, too, that he was fair to no man, and was no fairer to his friend than to his enemy.

On the morning of the fight they drove the Brown Bull into the Plain of Ai, and the Men of Erin sought the hills and the mountains from which to watch the battle between the bulls. When the two bulls caught sight of one another they stopped, and scraping the ground with their enormous hooves they threw up so many and such enormous sods over their shoulders that the day became dark and black as thunder. Their eyes blazed like balls of fire as they looked at one another, their cheeks and nostrils swelling and panting like the bellows in a blacksmith's forge. Then they ran at one another and began to gore each other and to butt their heads one against the other. And the clap and bang of one forehead hitting the other was like a sudden peal of thunder between high mountains. Then the White-Horned sunk his horns deep into the side of the Brown Bull, but the Brown pulled away and then chased the White-Horned, and Briciu, coming in between them, was knocked down and trampled thirty feet down into the earth.

So all day long the bulls butted and gored and chased each other till darkness came. Then the Men of Erin could see no longer, but they could hear the snorting and the blowing, the trampling and the bellowing of the maddened bulls as they fought all night over the whole country of Erin. North, south, east and west they went, and the whole country was ringing with their roaring and their snorting and their bellowing. And to this day wherever there is a Bulls' Stand, a Bulls' Gap, a Bulls' Ridge or a Bulls' Lock it was from that night when the Brown Bull of Cooley and the White-Horned Bull of Connacht fought all over Ireland. Early next morning at the first light the Men of Erin, who were waiting at Rath Cruachan with Ailell and Maeve, saw one of the bulls climb up on the ramparts of the royal rath, and he had a carcase impaled on his horns. The Men of Erin rose to see which of the bulls it was who had the victory. And Fergus cried out: 'Leave him have his victory, whichever one it is, and leave his trophy with him.' But when they discovered that it was the Brown Bull that had the White-Horned impaled on his horns, the Men of Erin rushed forward to make an end of him who had slain the White-Horned of Ailell.

But Fergus shouted out once more:

'I pledge my word that unless the spoils and fruits of victory are left with him and unless he is let go from here back to his own country peacefully, all that he has done to the vanquished bull will be as nothing to what slaughter I will do now.'

Then the Brown Bull gave out three of his loudest bellows, and the Men of Erin stayed quiet, for fear of what Fergus might do to them.

Turning eastwards to his own country then, the Brown Bull began on his journey home. But before he left the royal domain of Maeve, he tossed the liver of the White-Horned from his horns and left it in a heap in front of the palace, so that in this way Cruachan got its name—Cruac Aei meaning 'the heap of liver'.

Coming to the Shannon, he stopped to drink at the ford, and while he drank not one drop of the river passed him by. Then he tossed his horns again and the two loins of the White-Horned fell to the ground, giving the place its name to this day—Athlone, 'the ford of the loins'.

Shortly after this he stood on a high hill in the middle of Ireland and shook the remains of the White-Horned from his horns, sending the pieces flying in all directions, over the country, so that the hind leg landed in Waterford, 'the ford of the hind leg', and the ribs he sent hurtling up to Dublin, which is called 'the ford of the ribs' ever after.

Turning north, he came at last to his own country, and when he saw his native hills of Cooley once more, such joy and excitement rose up in him that he charged into a crowd of people that stood in his way and he killed every one of them.

Then the Brown Bull of Cooley turned his back on Erin and faced towards the north, and rushing at a high mountain that was in front of him, he drove his forehead at its great rocky flank, and a stream of red-black blood gushed out of his mouth, and his heart burst within him and he died.

# III

# THE FATE OF THE SONS OF USNACH

*(The third sorrow of story-telling)*

About the time when Cuchullin's name was in every mouth as the greatest hero of the Red Branch Knights, King Conor Mac Nessa sat one day at a banquet in the house of Fedlimid, his chief story-teller. And while the drinking-horns were passed around the board, and the men of poetry were singing their lays to the royal company, Fedlimid's wife gave birth to a daughter. When the birth was made known in the banqueting hall, Cathbad, the druid, rose and said that the new-born child would be called Deirdre, that she would have beauty beyond all telling, that kings and heroes would fight and kill one another for her favours, but that great ruin and evil would come to Ulster on her account.

'Let the maiden be put to death now,' said some of the young men of Ulster when they heard the forebodings of the druid.

But Conor answered: 'Not so, for I will take her and put her to fosterage in the lonely hills, where no eye but mine shall see her beauty, and in time she shall be my wife.'

And so it was that the child Deirdre was hidden away in a remote dwelling in the mountains, and there she was reared in charge of three persons only—a nurse, a teacher and a poetess named Lavarcham—and no other person save Conor himself was allowed to come near her dwelling. In this remote place among the hills she grew in years and in beauty until it was coming to the time when she would be ripe for marriage.

About this time one day Deirdre looked out through her window, and saw her foster-father skinning a calf upon the snow, in order to prepare a roast for her dinner. As the blood of the calf reddened the snow, a raven came down to drink it.

'Lavarcham,' said Deirdre, to the poetess who was by her side, 'that man only will I love who hath the three colours I see before me: the colour of the raven on his hair, the colour of the blood on his cheek, and the colour of the snow on his skin.'

'Truly,' said Lavarcham, 'there is such a one in the household of Conor this very day, and his name is Naisi, Son of Usnach.'

'If what you say is true, O Lavarcham, pray bring him to me in secret, for I shall never be in good health again until I see him.'

And Lavarcham whispered Deirdre's wish to Naisi, and he came one day in secret to the place where Deirdre was. As he stood alone in the plain, a little way from her dwelling, Deirdre flitted past him, and as he watched her and saw her great beauty, it came to his mind that she could be none other than Deirdre, whom Conor had hidden away from the eyes of all other men for fear of the strife her beauty might bring among them.

As Naisi stood and looked at Deirdre, love for her grew in his heart. And Deirdre herself knew that the warrior of the raven hair and of the glowing cheek before her must be Naisi of whom Lavarcham had spoken to her, and to whom she had already given her love.

As he looked at Deirdre, Naisi was dumb, for the power

of her beauty had taken his speech from him, and after that the fear of Conor's anger had kept him from speaking his love. But Deirdre knew no such fear, for never before had she seen anyone as young and as beautiful as Naisi, and her heart was filled with love. At a second glance Naisi's fear of Conor was overcome, and drawing close to her he asked her to fly with him from the wrath of Conor. Then they made a plan to leave at once with his brothers and their followers, and seek refuge outside the realm of Ulster and far from its king.

Naisi now gave his musical war-cry to call his brothers to him. When they came and heard of Naisi's and Deirdre's plan they warned him of Conor's anger:

'There shall come evil on thee from this, and thou shalt lie under a reproach of shame as long as thou dost live.'

But Naisi's love was stronger than all their fears, and they, seeing this, ceased to warn him, and the three took counsel together and decided to leave Ulster, taking Deirdre with them, and go into service with the other kings of Erin. So that night, taking with them three times fifty warriors, and the same number of women, the three brothers journeyed towards the south, and Deirdre bade farewell to Lavarcham and went with them. For a long time after leaving Ulster they travelled up and down through the country, homeless as the birds of the air, taking service now with this king and now with that, but all the time Conor's rage pursued them, until in the end no king or noble dared to give them shelter, for fear of the vengeance of the High King.

So it was that at last they had to leave the land of Erin and go to Scotland, and there in the wild glens they settled down, feeding themselves by what fell to their arms in the chase. After a time the three brothers offered their swords to the King of Scotland, and he was glad to take them into his service, for the fame of the valour of Naisi, Ainle and Ardan, the three Sons of Usnach, was well known to him. And for a while they remained with the King of Scotland, and won many battles for him against his enemies, but one day the King saw Deirdre and wished to make her his wife. Great anger seized Naisi when he heard this, and once again he and his brothers had to flee with Deirdre. This time they took refuge in a lonely island in the western seas.

Back in Erin, King Conor sat at a feast in the banqueting hall of the royal palace of Emain Macha. As he watched the wine-goblet circling freely among the warriors around his board, and listened to his men of music chanting their lays, the thoughts of the aged King strayed back to that other feast in the house of his story-teller, Fedlimid, many years before, when in the midst of such a scene as this Deirdre's birth had been announced, Deirdre, that child of such wild and wondrous beauty, the loss of whom had turned his heart to stone and had robbed him of such champions as Naisi, Ainle and Ardan. As his thoughts strayed over them he remembered the strange new tidings that had just come in from Scotland—of still another king desiring Deirdre for his own, and of the new exile of the Sons of Usnach in the desolate western isle. Conor felt the old jealousy surge over him again, and new thoughts of revenge began to slip into his brain. So above the sound of harp and tympan he raised his kingly voice, and called out to his assembled nobles and warriors of the Red Branch that he was willing to send a pardon to the Sons of Usnach and let them return to Ulster.

'Let messengers and envoys be sent for them into Alba [Scotland]' he said, 'and let one of their three dearest friends—Cuchullin, Conal Cearnach or Fergus Mac Roy—go with the messengers and pledge themselves to the Sons of Usnach that they can return in peace and safety.'

Great was the rejoicing among the Men of Ulster to hear this, and while rejoicing they praised the King for his generosity in pardoning the Sons of Usnach, and for allowing them to return to Ulster.

As Conor listened his eye wandered over the warriors of the Red Branch as they sat drinking their wine and speeding the mead cup around the table. His eagle eye picked out Fergus Mac Roy: Fergus the generous, the loyal, the warm-hearted. He beckoned to him and drew him apart, and told him privately to set out at once for Lough Etine, where Deirdre and Naisi were, and bring the royal pardon to the Sons of Usnach, and bid them and their followers return to Ulster with him:

'Set forward on thy way to-morrow, and bring them hither first to the fortress of Borach, by the edge of the Northern Sea, and now pledge thy word to me that whether they arrive in Erin by night or by day, neither stop nor stay be allowed them until they set foot here in Emain Macha before me.'

Fergus pledged his word to Conor that he would do his bidding, and he left the feast to prepare for his setting forth at the first light. Then Conor sought out Borach, son of Annte, and drawing him away from the banquet told him to return northward at once to his fortress, and have a feast prepared for Fergus by the time he would be coming back to Erin with the Sons of Usnach.

'Prepare this feast as for me,' said Conor, 'but bestow it upon Fergus, and he may not refuse it, since one of his bonds is never to refuse an invitation to a feast.'

And Conor, now having made sure that the Sons of Usnach would arrive back at Emain Macha without Fergus, their pledge of safety, sat once more at the banquet, and from that on no one was more mirthful, nor drank more deeply from the mead cup than he.

When Fergus came into the harbour of the Western Isle, near where the Sons of Usnach were said to be, he raised his voice and sent out a mighty shout over the land, and Naisi and Deirdre, who were seated together in their hunting-booth, playing chess, heard it.

'That is the cry of a Man of Erin,' said Naisi.

Deirdre, hearing it, knew it to be the cry of Fergus, and said, 'That is the cry of a Man of Alba,' for she feared the treachery of Conor, and did not want Naisi or his brothers to return to Erin ever again.

Again Fergus sent forth his cry, and Naisi said again: 'It is the cry of a Man of Erin.'

'Not so,' said Deirdre. 'Let us play on, for not unlike are the cries of a Man of Erin and a Man of Alba.'

But Fergus sent forth a third cry, and this time Naisi and his two brothers knew it to be the cry of Fergus. Naisi then told Ardan to go and meet Fergus and bring him to them. Ardan then went and brought Fergus back to Deirdre and Naisi, and they welcomed him lovingly, and asked for tidings from Erin.

'The tidings I have for you,' said Fergus, 'is that Conor has sent me to bring you a full pardon and to ask you to come back to Ulster. I have pledged my word with Conor to be your safeguard, and as I was ever loving and loyal to you, you should know that no harm will ever come to you while I am your surety.'

'Let us not leave Alba,' said Deirdre, and she brought up every reason that she could think of to prevent their going. Then, when she found that Naisi and his brothers were swayed by Fergus and were willing to return with him, she told them her dream:

'Three birds came to me in my sleep last night. Out of Emain Macha they came, and in their bills were three sips of honey. The three sips of honey they left with us, but they took with them three sips of our blood.'

The three brothers asked Deirdre to explain her dream, and she told them that the three sips of honey were the false messages of peace and pardon that Conor had given to Fergus for them. And the three sips of blood were the three Sons of Usnach who would be betrayed by Conor.

Hearing this, Fergus cried out aloud that he had pledged his word that if all the Men of Erin should betray them, he himself would fight for the Sons of Usnach against them all.

'We know it,' said Naisi, 'and we will go with you to Emain Macha.'

'And I will give you safe conduct every step of the way to the very footstool of Conor in his palace at Emain Macha,' said Fergus.

So there and then they prepared for their journey, and

taking Deirdre with them the three Sons of Usnach put themselves under the protection of Fergus, and set out on the sea westwards to Erin. And as they went, Deirdre, looking behind her at the coast of Scotland, made a lament to be leaving it.

'Beloved to me is that land to the East,
Alba with its marvels,
I would not have come hither from it
if I were not come with Naisi.

Beloved to me Dun Fidga and Dun Finn,
beloved the dun above them,
beloved Inis Draigen
and beloved Dun Sweeney.

Glen Laid!
I used to sleep there under the white rocks;
fish and flesh and rich badger
was my share in Glen Laid.

Glen Eitchi!
There I raised my first house,
delightful its wood, after rising,
a pen for the sun was Glen Eitchi.

Beloved is Draigen and its firm strand,
beloved its waters in pure sand:
I would not have come from the East
If I were not to come with my lover.'

As the Sons of Usnach touched the shores of Erin, Borach came down himself to meet and welcome them, and to invite Fergus to the feast he had prepared for him under the secret orders of Conor.

'And you cannot fail to come to this,' said Borach, 'for it is one of your prohibitions never to refuse a feast, and is is unlucky for a warrior to go against his prohibitions.'

When Fergus heard this he was sorely grieved. If he stayed for the feast he knew that the Sons of Usnach would have to journey on without him to King Conor and without his surety for their safety. And they could not wait for the feast, for he had pledged his word to the King

K·M

that they would make no stop, nor eat any food in Ireland until they would reach Emain Macha. In his dilemma Fergus turned to Naisi and asked what he should do.

Only Deirdre spoke: 'If you forsake the Sons of Usnach and consume the feast you will be paying a great price for it.'

'I will not forsake them,' said Fergus, 'for I will send my two sons with them, Illan the Fair and Buinne the Ruthless Red, and they will give them protection.'

Hearing this, Naisi and his brothers turned aside in anger, and said that from this on they would depend on their own arms to defend them, and leaving Fergus they made by the shortest way to Emain Macha. Illan the Fair and Buinne the Ruthless Red went with them. On the way Deirdre, now quite sure after their desertion by Fergus that Naisi and his brothers were lured to Ireland for their undoing, tried all her woman's persuasiveness to get Naisi to turn aside from Emain Macha and to cross the sea again to an island between Scotland and Ireland, and to remain there till Fergus had finished his feast and could give them safe conduct to Conor. But the sons of Fergus spoke up and said that their protection was as good as their father's, and that no harm would come to the Sons of Usnach while in their company. But as they journeyed on Deirdre continued to lament and to warn Naisi:

'My heart is a clot of sorrow this night,
And great is my shame and my grief,
To think that the three Sons of Usnach
In treacherous foes believe.'

But Naisi answering her told her not to be fearful, for his trust in Fergus, his ever loyal friend, was unshaken: for he knew that Fergus would not have come to Scotland to bring him and his brothers back to their deaths.

But as they drew near Emain Macha, Deirdre saw a cloud of blood forming over Naisi's head, and once again she begged him not to go on to Conor's palace:

'Rather let us go to Dun Dealgan, where Cuchullin

dwells, and stay there until Fergus shall come. Or else go to Emain under Cuchullin's protection.'

But again Naisi quieted her, and told her she should have no fear, since she was in the company of the bravest warriors of the land.

Then they drew near to Emain Macha, and Deirdre said to Naisi:

'If Conor invites you into the house where he dwells with his nobles and royal household he intends you no harm: but if he sends you to the House of the Red Branch Knights you may know that he has plotted treachery against you.'

No one answered Deirdre's warning, but the three Sons of Usnach strode bravely up to the Royal House and struck a loud blow thereon. The door-keeper took the news to Conor that the Sons of Usnach had come and stood waiting without. Conor drew apart and inquired of his servants if the House of the Red Branch was victualled with food and drink. They answered that there was food and drink for the five battalions of Ulster there if they came for it.

'If that be so,' said Conor, 'let the Sons of Usnach be taken into it.'

'Come, Naisi,' said Deirdre, when she heard this, 'let us fly even now, before the vengeance of Conor falls on us at last.'

But Illan the Fair, son of Fergus, spoke again:

'Great is the fear and the cowardice you would have us show, girl, in urging that we flee before even one blow has been aimed at us. Let us go to the House of the Red Branch,' he said, 'as Conor has asked.'

'To the House of the Red Branch we will go,' said Naisi, and he led the way.

As they sat there under Conor's roof servants were sent to wait on them and on their followers; and sweet-tasting wines and the most delicate and tender viands were put before them. But neither Deirdre nor the Sons of Usnach broke their fast, so weary were they after their journey over the Northern Sea. Then Naisi said they would play chess and called for a chess-board.

After a while Conor called Lavarcham, Deirdre's old nurse, to him, and bade her go to Deirdre and see if she still had the same beauty of face and form, or if time and the unsettled life of fleeting from one place to another had robbed her of that beauty which was not to be found in any woman of the race of Adam.

Lavarcham went to the House of the Red Branch and found Deirdre and Naisi playing chess. As she looked at them and at Ardan and Ainle, she broke into a shower of tears, for Naisi and Deirdre and after them their two brothers were dearer to Lavarcham than anyone in the whole world, and she knew that Conor had treachery in his heart towards them.

Kissing each one of them lovingly and fondly many times, she spoke to Naisi and his brothers:

'It is not wise of you, my beloved children, to have with you, while you are in his power, a precious jewel that the King most covets.'

Then she told the sons of Fergus to bar and bolt the doors and windows, and to prepare to defend themselves. And she took leave of them sorrowfully, and went back to Conor.

'I have bad tidings for you, O King,' she said when she went back to the house of Conor. 'It is that the form and features of her that was the most beautiful woman in the whole world are now no longer the same, for she has lost her beauty.'

When Conor heard Lavarcham utter these words his bitterness and rage went from him, and he called for his goblet to be filled with wine and he sat drinking among his nobles. But as he drank, a man whose father had been killed by Naisi passed by the table, and his desire for revenge was rekindled. He called Trendhorn to him, for it was he who was the sworn enemy of Naisi, and he asked him to go to the House of the Red Branch and to bring him back news of Deirdre. Trendhorn went and all the Ulstermen held silent, for Conor's treacherous plan was now plain to them all. Finding the doors bolted, Trendhorn fled from window to window, but they were shuttered and he could not even look in. Looking up, he saw a small window high in the wall under the eaves, and climbing to that he found he could look down at Deirdre and Naisi and watch them as they played at chess. Chancing to glance up at the window, Deirdre saw the black, intent eye of Trendhorn as he watched them. She looked away, pretending not to have seen, but she contrived to touch Naisi's hand as he was moving his chess-man. Naisi looked up and saw Trendhorn, and taking up a chess-man, threw it with such force against the window that it knocked out his enemy's eye.

Full of rage and fury, Trendhorn now ran back to Conor and told him that the beauty of Deirdre was still without peer; 'and as she sits there among the three Sons of Usnach they bear themselves as proudly as kings, and Naisi, with her by his side, is like the king of the whole world.'

Furiously jealous, Conor now got together a band of hirelings, since none of the Ulstermen would go against the Sons of Usnach for him, and he ordered the hirelings to attack the House of the Red Branch and to capture Naisi and his brothers. They set forth then and attacked the House on all sides, but though there were fully fifty of them against Naisi and his brothers and the two sons of Fergus, they could not come nearer than an arrow-flight to its walls. Then they withdrew, but under cover of darkness they crept back, and building walls of faggots and dry kindling around it they tried to set it ablaze.

Seeing this, Buinne and his followers rushed out, and, quenching the flames, slew many of the attackers and drove the rest away. Conor then, seeing the failure of his attack, sought a parley with Buinne, and offered as a bribe a cantred of land if he would desert the Sons of Usnach. Buinne took the cantred of land from Conor and basely broke his pledge with Naisi and his brothers.

Conor now mustered another band of hirelings, and sent

them against the House of the Red Branch once more. But Illan, the second son of Fergus, greatly ashamed of his brother's treachery, now came out against the hirelings, and killing many of them, drove off the others in disorderly flight.

Conor then armed his son Fiacha with his own chosen arms and sent him against Illan. It was a fierce fight, but Illan at last overcame Fiacha, who had to crouch for protection under his father's shield, which moaned when its owner was in danger. Away in the south of Ulster, the champion Conal Cearnach heard the moaning of Conor's shield, and thinking his King was in danger, he rushed to the fray. Not waiting to see who his opponent was, he attacked Illan and gave him his death-blow.

'Alas, Conal,' said Illan with his dying breath, 'it is a bad deed you have done to slay Illan your friend, who was fighting to protect the Sons of Usnach from the deadly treachery of Conor.'

Conal, full of grief and rage when he found he had killed Illan, struck off the head of Fiacha and left the contest. Then as the last weakness came over Illan he threw his arms into the House of the Red Branch, and called on Naisi to fight valiantly.

Now the three Sons of Usnach agreed among themselves that each of them should keep guard a third of the night. So when darkness set in and Conor's hirelings renewed the attack, Ardan came out of the house, and with a gallant band put them to flight. The three brothers now decided to go out together with the remnant of their men and fight their way to a place of safety. So, linking their shields together, Naisi and his brothers put Deirdre between them, and they bounded out over the walls of Emain, slaying three hundred of the attackers.

Conor, seeing his hirelings defeated, called for a parley, and offered Naisi and his brothers peace and their places in the Red Branch Knights if they would lay down their arms and submit to him.

Believing his word, Naisi and his brothers thereupon

laid down their arms, and went to the King to make their submission. But no sooner did he see them disarmed than Conor had them seized and bound, and called for volunteers among the Ulstermen to put them to death. But not one among the Ulstermen could be got to carry out the King's treacherous design. Among the hirelings, however, was one called Maine Red-Hand, son of the King of Norway, and because his father and two brothers had fallen by the hand of Naisi, he was willing to put the Sons of Usnach to death.

'Let me be the first to be slain,' said Ardan, for he did not wish to see his brothers killed.

'Not so,' said Ainle; 'let me be first.'

'We three shall die together at the one blow,' said Naisi, 'so that neither shall see the other beheaded.'

So Naisi took his own sword—the sword given him by Manannan Mac Lir, the sea-god, the sword that never left the leavings of a blow behind it—and he gave it to Maine Red-Hand. Then Naisi, Ainle and Ardan stretched out their necks side by side on the one block. And Maine raised the sword and struck off their heads with a single blow.

When Deirdre saw this she threw herself on her knees by the side of their bodies, and uttered a sorrowful lament. Then she sank down beside Naisi and died.

# IV

## THE DEATH OF CUCHULLIN

FOR seven years after the routing of her armies by Cuchullin and the Ulstermen, at the time of the Cattle Raid of Cooley, Maeve did not once raise a hand against Ulster. But the proud Queen never forgot the disgrace put on her at that time by Cuchullin, when he held back the Men of Erin all through the long winter when there was not a warrior in Ulster who could have lifted a spear against her. She knew, too, that as long as Cuchullin was alive she could never go against her ancient enemies in the North. So she set to work to bring him to his death.

She first gathered around her as allies all Cuchullin's foes, men whose fathers or brothers he had slain, and men who were jealous or envious of him or of Ulster. She sent secret messengers from one end of the country to the other, seeking these enemies of Cuchullin, whispering revenge in their ears, and promising great rewards and spoils to any man who would help her to destroy him.

As well as these mortal warriors who joined Maeve in her vengeful schemes were the six children of Celatin the wizard, whom Cuchullin had slain with his twenty-seven sons when he was keeping Maeve's army out of Ulster. This monstrous brood of six—three sons and three daughters—were born at one birth to Celatin's wife when she heard that Cuchullin had killed her husband. Maeve took the six ill-shapen, evil-looking beings and reared them herself for her own ends, and kept them by her until they were of an age to travel. Then she sent them east to Babylon, and to Alba and throughout the wide world to learn magical arts and spells so as to destroy Cuchullin. They studied from dawn till dark and from dark till dawn with all the famous wizards of the east, and even made their way to the fearful realm of the underground, where they met Vulcan. Vulcan, with his own hand, forged and tempered for them three spears, three swords and three knives. Into these he put all the cruel venom and poison known to him, and so deadly were they that no one could escape death if they but touched his skin and drew one drop of his blood.

'Take these weapons,' said Vulcan to the children of Celatin, 'and guard them well; for three kings will die by them, and one of the kings will be that king among warriors, among champions, among heroes, that king of bravery who was never yet defeated, that hard-hitting, noble youth known to you as "The Hound of Ulster".'

So at last, with loud and raucous shouts of delight, the mis-shapen brood sat up on the lap of the East Wind and set off on the long voyage to Erin, until at Samain time, when summer's end had come, they floated down on the broad ramparts of Maeve's palace at Cruachan.

Maeve, seeing her six hideous servants, opened her casements and bade them enter. With joy she heard them give an account of their seven years of learning among the wizards of the east. She heard how they could make the leaves and the wisps of hay, blown along the ground by the autumn wind, take on the appearance of an invading army; of how they could fill the land with smoke and fire and with the clash and noise of battle; and how in the calm of a summer's day they could raise up the appearance of a storm on dry land with mountainous seas threatening to swallow all before them. Lastly they drew out from under their capes the deadly knives and spears and swords that Vulcan had fashioned for them, showed them to Maeve, and told her that in each one the smithy of the underworld had put the killing of a king; and in particular he had put the killing of that hateful hewer and hacker of Connachtmen —' The Hound of Ulster '.

' That is well indeed,' said Maeve. ' Go forth and destroy him.'

Seating themselves once more high up on the lap of the wind, the six monstrous goblins flew up over Ulster, and they peered and pried into every dun and palace, until they found Cuchullin, who was at this time at home in Dun Dealgan, with Emir, his wife. Seeing him they at once set about filling the land of Muirthemne, Cuchullin's own patrimony, with the smoke and noise of war and hostings, the clashing of steel on steel, the neighing of horses and the screams and cries of women, in order to draw the champion of Ulster out to battle for his province.

But at the first sign of the witchery of Celatin's brood, Emir, his wife, and Cathbad the druid and Niav the wife of Cuchullin's best warrior friend, Conal of the Victories, and all his other good friends gathered around him and prayed him not to be lured out to his destruction by these sights and sounds of war, which, they told him, were but the spells and visions raised up around him by his enemies. Instead they persuaded him to go with them to the Glen of the Deaf, in Donegal, where these sounds and allurements could not reach him. There, in this lonely and peaceful glen, his friends kept him company, and he gave his word to Niav that he would not leave them without her permission. Then they sang songs and played sweet music to soothe his spirit and to bring him forgetfulness; and in playing chess and telling old tales they passed the time pleasantly till the power of the children of Celatin would be at an end. For Cuchullin's friends knew that this power of raising up magical visions around him could only last for three days.

All this time the goblin brood, knowing that their three days were running out, were sailing on the wind up over Ulster, searching for Cuchullin. They peered into every glen and wooded place where he might be hiding, but nowhere could they see any sign of him, until on the third day one of the goblin women wafted herself up on to the highest cloud in the heavens, from where she could cast her eye over the whole of Ulster's land. As she peered and searched, it seemed to her that the sounds of lutes and the joyous laughter of maidens came to her ears from the farthest dim tip of the land. Changing herself at once into a raven, she flew straight to the lonely mountain valley. There, in a fold among the high mountains, she saw a beautiful summer palace, and on the sunny bawn in front of the palace she saw Cuchullin seated among his musicians, his dancing-maidens and his men of poetry.

Once again she changed her shape—this time she took on the form of one of Niav's hand-maidens. In this disguise she drew a little near to the group around Cuchullin, and calling her mistress aside, on some clever pretext, sent her into a nearby wood, where she put a spell of straying on her. Then, taking on the shape of Niav herself, she went back to Cuchullin and told him that the Men of Erin were invading his country, and were at that very moment burning Dun Dealgan and driving off his cattle and herds, and she begged him to go before it was too late and drive them out.

At once Cuchullin rose up, and taking his arms ordered Laegh his charioteer to get his horses and to prepare his chariot. At this his friends all crowded around him and began to plead with him not to be drawn out by the magical visions made by his enemies, and Cathbad the druid made a pledge to him that if he would stay with them but one more day he would be free for ever from the spells of Celatin's brood. But madness had seized Cuchullin's brain, and he believed now that his enemies were ravaging the province and that he must rush forth at once to defend it. So he thrust his friends aside.

Then Emir came to him and begged him not to be deluded by these visions:

'These phantom armies that you see now around the ramparts of the palace are nothing but the dry leaves of autumn blown by the wind.'

But Cuchullin bade her not to hold him back from his fate.

'Fame outlasts life,' he told her, 'and life itself would be but a poor thing if it were bought with my dishonour. For dishonoured I would be if I did not go forth now and defend Ulster against my enemies.'

Laegh then went to yoke Cuchullin's steed, the Grey of Macha, but the horse fled both from him and from Cuchullin, and when at last they captured him and led him to the chariot, great tears of blood trickled from his eyes. It was another sign of doom that when Cuchullin mounted his chariot, his foot had no sooner touched the floor than all his weapons fell from their wonted places and crashed around his feet. And Laegh turned pale to see them fall.

Cuchullin now drove off southward, and as he drove, it seemed to him that out before him, line after line, his enemies were drawn up in battle array, and the clash and din of warfare on every side deafened his ears and clouded his brain. He thought, too, that he saw the palace of Emain covered with a pall of smoke, and lit up by huge tongues of flame, and that from the ramparts he saw the burning corpse of Emir tossed out headless before him. In another vision he saw his own fort, Dun Dealgan, destroyed by fire, while shrieking women fled helpless from its flaming towers. And in all the countryside he saw the Men of Erin burning, killing and destroying, and no hand raised to stop them.

On their way they passed over a stream. There they saw a maiden kneeling by a ford, washing the clothes and fighting-gear of a warrior, and as she washed, the water ran red with blood. Seeing Cuchullin, she drew a blood-stained corslet out of the water, and held it up. Looking at it he knew it for his own.

'Who is this woman?' he asked his charioteer.

'That is the Washer of the Ford, O Cuchullin,' said Laegh. 'She is the daughter of the goddess of war, and she washes the garments and armour of those about to die. O Cuchullin, let us turn aside while there is yet time, for it seems to me that it is thy sword and thy corslet that dyes the water red.'

But Cuchullin answered:

'I would gladly toss my life to the goddess of war if once again I could work havoc on the Men of Erin, and drive them out of Ulster.'

Then he drove on till he came to the enemy hosts that Maeve had collected near the border for the invasion of the North. Three times he drove through them, cutting them down and leaving them in little heaps on each side of his tracks. Then he performed his three Thunder Feats, rushing through them in his roaring chariot till their bones flew apart and with the lightning of his blades scattered them broadcast on the wide plain of Muirthemne, like the sands of the sea or the stars in the frosty heavens. And his wheels and his horses' hooves ground them like hailstones under a millstone.

Twice the Men of Erin broke under the fury of his attack. Twice Erc son of Cairpre rallied them again. Then, like a god, his chargers breathing fire, his sword white-hot in his hand, Cuchullin drove at the enemy for the third time, and this time they fled beyond recall, for neither Erc, nor Luga, nor Curoi, Cuchullin's bitterest foes, could halt them as they fled before his onset. But at the very moment when the rout was at its height there came a noise of screaming down the wind, as the six children of Celatin entered into the fight with their hideous cries. They thrust Vulcan's deadly weapons into the hands of Erc and Luga and Curoi and bade them put an end to their enemy.

Erc eagerly took the weapons of death. He turned and faced Cuchullin. He took careful aim. Then he threw the venomous spear. It glanced off Cuchullin and plunged its head deep into the breast of his faithful charioteer.

Cuchullin tore at the spear to rend it from the flesh of his friend, but no strength could stir the barb one hair's-breadth from its deadly grip. Heedless of his enemies, each with his spear poised to strike, Cuchullin bent over the dying Laegh, and bidding him a tender farewell gently laid him down.

Again he turned to the hosts and, fury-driven, he hacked and hewed around him in savage revenge for Laegh. But now Luga unloosed another barb upon him, and this time it pierced the Grey of Macha and sent the horse stumbling to the ground. Unyoking him, Cuchullin sent him aside from the thick of the fighting, and he galloped off with Vulcan's spear stuck deep in his flesh.

For the third time Cuchullin faced his enemies on the great Plain of Muirthemne. Once more he dashed at them and mowed down great swathes in their lines; and once more they fled before him. And then the goblin brood of Celatin shrieked at Curoi to use the third spear of Vulcan before it would be too late.

'A king,' they shrieked, 'must fall by that spear.'

'I heard you say a king would fall by the spear of Erc this morning,' he answered them.

'It is true,' they intoned. 'Two kings have already fallen by Vulcan's spears—Laegh the King of Charioteers, and the Grey of Macha, the King of Steeds. By this one will fall the King of Champions, Ulster's glorious Hound.'

Curoi raised his spear, and taking long and careful aim he threw it at Cuchullin. The bright steel flew up into the air. In the sun it flashed its blue wing. Then down it drove straight for Cuchullin's side, and sank itself deep in his flesh until his blood gushed out upon the floor of the chariot. As Cuchullin fell, his one remaining horse, the Black Sainglend, broke away and fled, with the wrecked chariot hanging from his gory back.

Cuchullin now sank slowly to the ground. Seeing him stretched, with his life-blood flowing from him in a stream, the enemy hosts stealthily crept back. They stood in a

wide circle around him, their weapons grounded, and in silence they watched the champion die.

Then Cuchullin spoke to his enemies, saying:

'I would fain quench my thirst at the lakeside.'

To this the Men of Erin answered that they gave him leave to go. So, rising to his feet and with his hands holding the great wound in his side to halt the blood, he went to the brink of the lake and drank, and washing himself in the water, he prepared himself to die. A little way from the lake he saw a standing pillar, and going to it he stood up straight with his back against it, facing his enemies, and throwing his girdle around the stone behind him, he tied it around his breast, so that he might die standing upright.

All the while his enemies stood around him in a wide circle, still afraid to come too near while life remained in him.

The hero's blood had by this formed a channel down into the lake; as Cuchullin watched it flow he saw an otter creep out from some nearby bushes and timidly lap his blood. Tugging the spear-shaft from his wound he threw it at the beast, and sent him scampering away. Then a raven stealthily hopped up and dipped its beak in the stream of his blood; but so greedy was it to drink that its claws got entangled in some weed, and it fell head foremost into the red pool. Cuchullin laughed a loud and hearty laugh, for he knew it would be the last laugh he would ever give.

His head now sank slowly on his breast. And at the last, as he stood there facing his enemies, on the Great Plain of Muirthemne, his life-blood trickling from him, the great sky of Ireland over him, the Hero Light about his head grew dim and slowly died. At that the last bright ray of life went out of Cuchullin, and he gave a sigh so deep and strong that it split the pillar-stone behind him.

It was then that Luga, seeing the Hero Light fade and die, drew near to Cuchullin, and made to take the hero's head from his body. But as he did so, the sword fell from the champion's upraised arm, and struck the hand of Luga to the ground.

## V

# KING FERGUS MAC LEIDE AND THE WEE FOLK

At the time of Cuchullin it happened there was a king in Ulster called Fergus Mac Leide, who was also known as Fergus Wryneck from a wound he had received in an encounter with a horrible river-monster, who lived in a lake near his castle. Now, a few years after Fergus had received this blemish from the river-monster it happened that, away in the Land of the Leprechauns, Iubadan, their King, held a banquet for the nobles and fighting men of his land, the Land of the Wee Folk. To the feast came all his champion fighting men, the greatest of whom, Glower, could hew down a thistle with but one blow of his sword, and in a wrestling match could not be thrown by less than twelve of his brother champions. To the feast also came the King's chief bard, Eisirt, Beg, the King's son and heir, Bevo, Iubadan's Queen, and all her chief women-in-waiting, and all the notables of the court.

Iubadan was careful to seat all his guests in order of rank —Bevo on his right hand, Eisirt on his left. At the other side of the hall and facing him sat his son Beg with the great chiefs and nobles of the land. Glower, his strong man, stood at his undisputed place of honour at the door-post of the house, to keep the door and to protect all within.

Now, all being seated, the feast went ahead. The wine-bearers drew the spigots from the wine-vats of red yew. Carvers stood carving by the great sizzling haunches of roast hare and rabbit. Field-mice and robins were taken down from the spits, and scullions ran backwards and forwards with jugs of old ale and mead. Soon the hall was buzzing with sounds of merry talk and laughter, as the wine-cups passed and goblets were drained. Then, when at last the mirthful company had done ample justice to the great haunches of roast hare and rabbit, and when nothing remained of the juicy field-mice and robins but the white bones that were being noisily crunched by the mastiffs under the table, King Iubadan rose to his feet and, holding on high his great jewel-studded goblet, that was as large as any acorn that grew in the forests of Erin, he toasted the company gathered before him. And as his eye roved over the brave and noble gathering, his heart within him swelled with pride, and he said:

'Has anyone here before me ever seen a king mightier than myself?'

And with one voice the noble company answered: 'Never, O King.'

'And tell me,' he called aloud, 'is there in all the world a strong man the equal of my strong man Glower?'

'There is not in truth, O King,' they answered.

'And,' he shouted, louder than ever, 'it is beyond yea or nay the truth that nobody in the whole Eastern or Western Worlds would think of coming into this, our land, to take captives, or hostages, for there is in no part of the Eastern or Western Worlds any champions or warriors that could stand up to the champions and warriors of this, the Land of the Wee Folk.'

And here the King paused to hear the people agree with him once more, but just as he paused a single peal of laughter broke out, that rippled in the rafters over his head, and terrified each and every one of the noble company around him.

The King, looking around him in anger and surprise, was just in time to see Eisirt, his chief poet and bard of the land, in an uncontrollable fit of laughter.

Choking with anger, and in a voice like the thunder heard in a sea-shell, the King demanded of Eisirt:

'Why dost thou laugh so, Eisirt, I pray thee?'

'I laugh to hear thee say that thy warriors are so powerful,' said Eisirt. 'Why, there is a province in Erin, called Ulster, and one warrior from there would go single-handed through thy four battalions, and scatter them as a hawk would scatter a flock of starlings.'

'Seize him!' shouted the King. 'Seize the scornful poet, and put him into the deepest dungeon. He shall pay dearly for his foolish words.'

Rushing forward, Iubadan's soldiers put Eisirt in shackles, and dragged him quickly from the hall. But before he left the door, he turned back, and begged the King to give him a chance to prove the truth of what he had said.

'Give me but a few days, O King, and I shall myself go to Ulster, to the house of King Fergus Mac Leide, and from there I shall bring back some token that will prove to thee that what I have said about the warriors of Ulster is true.'

'It shall be as thou sayest, but remember, if thou dost not bring me back proof, to the dungeon with thee for evermore!' said the King.

So the guards set Eisirt free, and he went at once to his chamber to get ready for the journey, putting on a shirt of finest white silk, sewn with gold thread, his gold-embroidered tunic, his scarlet cloak and his shoes of white bronze. Then he set forth, taking the straightest and shortest road to Emmania, the royal palace of King Fergus Mac Leide, King of Ulster.

When he appeared before the door of the royal palace of Emmania he shook his poet's rod, so that all the gold and silver bells on it made a musical chime. The gate-keeper, throwing back the great door, beheld on the ground a very small man—so small that the close-cropped grass, amid which he stood, came up to his waist. Looking closer, the gate-keeper saw that the wee man had a noble bearing, was dressed in princely raiment, and that his hair had the poet's plaiting on it. The gate-keeper, full of astonishment at such an unusual visitor, went to King Fergus with all haste to tell him of the wee man who wished to speak to him.

'Is he as small as my dwarf, Hugh?' asked King Fergus, pointing to his chief poet, who sat beside him, and who was so small that he could sit comfortably on the outstretched palm of a fully grown man.

'He is so small,' said the gate-keeper, 'that he could stand on the palm of Hugh himself and would have plenty of room.'

When they heard this the whole assembly broke into loud laughter, and demanded to see the wee visitor at once. And so great was their curiosity that they all left the festive table, at which they had been sharing a banquet with the King, and trooped out to the gate on the rampart to see Eisirt for themselves. But seeing this great crowd of enormous giants coming towards him, and then making a circle around him, Eisirt called out to them to keep back from him:

'Huge men, do not come near me, for I fear that your breaths, like great stormy winds, would blow me off my feet. But let that small man yonder bear me in to safety, that I may speak with your King and tell him who I am, and whence I have come.'

Hugh the dwarf then took the little man, and, gently placing him on the palm of his hand, bore him into the banqueting hall, and all the guests once more took their places at the table, and the feast went ahead again.

Eisirt, on being placed on the table, told the King that he was the chief poet of the Leprechauns, and that he was the bearer of greetings from his King, Iubadan, King of the Land of the Wee Folk, to King Fergus Mac Leide of Ulster. Then Fergus ordered that the little man be served immediately with food and drink, but before the server could do the King's bidding, Eisirt called out:

'Do not set either food or drink before me, for I will neither eat of your food nor drink of your wine.'

To which King Fergus made answer:

'A very uncivil speech that is, in truth. And to teach him better manners let him be dropped into a goblet of wine, so that whether he likes to or not, he may drink a little of our mellowing wine.'

So, seizing Eisirt, a cup-bearer dropped him into a goblet

of wine, and Eisirt was compelled to keep swimming round and round on its surface, while all the guests watched him with much amusement.

'Men of Ulster,' Eisirt now called out, as he gasped and spluttered in the wine-goblet, 'lift me out of here, for there is much wisdom and knowledge I can give you, if you suffer me not to be drowned.'

'Let us have some of that knowledge,' they all shouted.

Then Eisirt began to reveal the secrets of each one in turn beginning with the King. But before he had gone far, each one, fearing what hidden sin of his Eisirt was going to make public, shouted: 'Enough, enough; take him out and let him be.' So they lifted him out of the wine-goblet and dried him with silk napkins.

'Now, Eisirt,' said the King, 'if you are a poet, let us hear one of your lays.'

Eisirt then recited a poem for King Fergus, and when it was ended the King and all his company praised it, and proclaimed Eisirt a true poet, and heaped gold and jewels and silver ornaments on him as a reward for his poem. Piled up around him on the table, they hid Eisirt completely from view, and made a prisoner of him, so that he cried out to them to take away their gifts:

'Good people, I thank you for your generosity, but I must beg you to take them back, for in the land of Faylinn, from which I come, there is no man short of such things.'

But the royal company refused, saying that never did they, nor never would they, take back a reward once they had given it. So Eisirt then begged them to divide the precious things between the bards and the learned men of Ulster, 'and', he bade them, 'do not forget the horse-boys and the jesters. I would fain have one third of the whole divided among them.'

At the end of three days Eisirt said he would return to his own country. Hugh the Bard, hearing him, said he would like to go with him for a short visit, and see his King and his people. And Eisirt, glad that Hugh would bear him company, said:

'Glad am I that thou hast chosen to come with me of thine own will, for if I bade thee come, and if a kind welcome be given to thee, thou will think it is but the due of a bidden guest, but seeing that thou comest of thine own free will, thou wilt perchance be pleased.'

So Eisirt and Hugh fared forth together to the Land of the Leprechauns. And walking beside Eisirt, Hugh the Dwarf, who in Ulster could sit comfortably on the palm of any fully grown man, now towered like a giant above his companion, and his step, being as long as ten of Eisirt's, made it difficult for them to keep pace with one another, so that Hugh said to the wee poet: 'Eisirt, thou art but a poor walker.' So Eisirt now and again took a fit of running till he was an arrow's flight in front of Hugh, and in this way they kept going till they reached the Strand of the Strong Men by the sea.

'How are we going to cross the sea?' asked Hugh.

'The steed of Iubadan will bear us both lightly over the water,' said Eisirt. And after a short wait on the beach they saw a small animal come skipping over the waves towards them.

'There is a hare coming towards us now,' said Hugh.

'Not a hare, but the horse of Iubadan,' said Eisirt.

And as it came up close to them, Hugh saw that it had two flashing eyes, a long crimson mane and a tail of golden curls. Eisirt mounted and invited Hugh to sit up behind him. But Hugh grumbled and said the horse was only just strong enough for Eisirt himself. 'Stop fault-finding,' said Eisirt, 'and you will find that neither yourself, nor the weight of your wisdom will bear our steed down.'

So Hugh got up behind Eisirt and they rode off lightly over the crests of the billows, and in no time had crossed the sea. Then the fairy steed, shaking the spray from his hooves, pranced up on dry land on the shores of Faylinn, where a great crowd of the Wee People were gathered to meet them.

'Here comes Eisirt and an enormous giant along with him,' they shouted as they saw him come.

Iubadan went forward to welcome Eisirt and to hear his news.

'But why bring with you this giant to destroy us?' he asked as he kissed him.

'No giant is he,' said Eisirt, 'but the chief poet of Ulster and the King's dwarf. In the land from which he comes he is indeed the smallest, so that he can stand on the outstretched palm of any grown man.' And while they wondered at Hugh's great size Eisirt said to the King:

'Now, O King, that I have returned and brought with me a small token of the giant size of all Ulster's warriors, I challenge thee to go thyself to Ulster and to taste the royal porridge that is made nightly for King Fergus Mac Leide.'

Hearing this, the King of the Wee Folk was in great dismay, and went to his Queen Bevo and told her that Eisirt had challenged him to go to the Land of the Giants, and bade her be ready to bear him company.

'I shall do as you say, my Lord, but it was not a wise or just thing to have cast Eisirt into prison.'

So, mounting on a golden, fairy steed, Iubadan and his Queen crossed the seas to Ulster, and that night, while everyone lay sound asleep, they entered the royal palace of Fergus unseen by all.

'Iubadan,' said Bevo, 'make haste and search for the porridge that Eisirt wishes you to taste, and let us depart again, before the giants awaken.'

So, entering the kitchens of the palace, they found the great porridge pot, that to Iubadan and Bevo was an enormous giant's cauldron, but on no account could Iubadan reach the top of it to look in, not to mind to taste it.

'Stand up on thy horse,' said Bevo.

This he did, and now he saw the porridge half-way down, with the silver spoon standing up in it. But alas! his arm would not reach the handle of the spoon. He struggled and he stretched, he balanced and he swayed and he almost reached it when he fell, up to his waist, into the porridge.

Seeing him fall, Bevo cried out in despair, and chid him for his rashness in getting himself into this trouble. And Iubadan, to comfort her, said:

'Rash indeed I was, but do not stay by me, since you can do nothing to aid me now. Take the horse and depart from here before the day breaks.'

But Bevo would not leave him yet awhile: 'I will not go from hence until I see what is going to happen to thee.'

When the day dawned, the scullions on rising found Iubadan in the porridge pot, at which they greatly laughed and wondered. And picking him out, they bore him and Bevo off to the King.

'By my faith,' said King Fergus, 'here we have two others of the Wee Folk come to visit us. Who art thou, Wee Man, and who is that by thy side?'

'I am King of the Wee Folk, and this is my wife Bevo,' said Iubadan.

'Take them away and keep a close eye on them,' said Fergus, 'for I fear that the people of Faery are laying some mischievous plot, or why else would they send their messengers thither?'

'Do not send us among the common rough people of thy household, O King, for we would greatly suffer from their rough and churlish manners and ways, and I give you my kingly word that we shall never go from hence without thy knowledge.'

Fergus had them set apart then in one of his own rooms, and gave them a serving-man to wait on them. To make them comfortable the serving-man set about kindling a fire for them, throwing upon the blaze a twig that had some woodbine twisted around it. Iubadan, seeing the woodbine, picked the twig from the fire, and in a poem he gave the serving-man advice on the woods that he was to burn and the woods he was not to burn from that on—

'WOODS TO BURN AND WOODS NOT TO BURN

O man that for Fergus of the Feasts dost kindle fire,
Whether afloat or ashore burn not the king of woods.

Monarch of Innishfail's forests the woodbine is, whom none may hold captive;
No feeble sovereign's effort is it to hug all tough trees in his embrace.

The pliant woodbine if thou burn, wailings for misfortune will abound,
Dire extremity at weapons' points or drowning in great waves will follow.

Burn not the precious apple-tree of spreading and low-sweeping bough;
Tree ever decked in bloom of white, against whose fair head all men put forth the hand.

The surly blackthorn is a wanderer, a wood that the artificer burns not;
Throughout his body, though it be scanty, birds in their flocks warble.

The noble willow burn not, a tree sacred to poems;
Within his bloom bees are a-sucking; all love the little cage.'

And so Iubadan and his Queen Bevo lived in Erin, and Fergus and his Court delighted in the Wee Man's songs and in his lays, and he and his Queen too seemed happy among the giants. But one day the seven battalions of the Wee Folk, determined to get back their King and Queen, appeared on the bawn outside the royal palace. Fergus and his nobles went out to confer with them.

'Give us back our King,' they cried, 'and we will gladly pay a ransom.'

'What ransom will you pay?' asked Fergus.

'We will cover this vast plain with corn every year without your having to plough or sow it.'

'I will not give up Iubadan for that,' said Fergus.

'Then to-night we will do thee a great mischief.'

'What mischief?'

'We shall loose all the calves of Ulster to their mothers, so that they shall drink their milk, and by morning there will not be enough milk in the province to feed one babe.'

'I will not release Iubadan for that,' said the King.

Then they threatened to defile every lake and well in Ulster.

'Not even for that will I release Iubadan,' said Fergus.

The Wee Folk went off then and defiled the wells, the lakes and the rivers, and once more came back and demanded Iubadan.

'To-night we will burn all the mill-beams of the province.'

'That,' said Fergus, 'is but a puny mischief and merits not Iubadan.'

'We will wreak vengeance on thee unless thou givest back Iubadan.'

'What vengeance?'

'We will cut off the ears of every blade of corn in your kingdom.'

'I shall not give up Iubadan.'

They went then and snipped off every ear of corn from one end of the kingdom to the other, and coming back to Emmania once more they threatened:

'We will take the hair from every man and every woman in your kingdom so that it will never grow again and for evermore they will be covered with reproach and shame.'

'If you do that,' said Fergus, 'I give you my word I will slay Iubadan.'

Iubadan, hearing this, begged to be allowed to speak to his people, and Fergus granting his request, he appeared before them. Seeing him approach, and thinking he had been released, they set up a cheer of triumph and victory. But Iubadan, speaking to them, told them they must go home quietly, as Fergus was not yet of mind to release him, and before going they should undo all the wrong they had done.

Then the Wee Folk departed, and when they had gone, Iubadan, sick at heart with longing for his country and his people, went to Fergus and said:

'What treasure of all my treasures will you take and let me go?'

'Name for me your primest treasures,' said Fergus.

Iubadan then told Fergus about his spear, that in battle was a match for hundreds; his shield, that protected its owner from all wounds and hurts; his belt, which protected its wearer from all sickness; his cauldron, which, if stones were put into it, would turn out meat fit for kings; his swine, that though killed and eaten today yet to-morrow are alive again; his shoes of white bronze, that allow the wearer to walk on the sea as if it were on dry land, and many other treasures of wondrous virtue.

Fergus pondered on all these magic things, but he made up his mind that the one treasure that he desired above all others was a pair of the magic shoes that permitted their wearer to walk on the water as if he were on dry land. And these shoes he took as Iubadan's ransom, and gave leave to the King of the Wee Folk and his wife to return home to their people.

For Fergus remembered the river-monster and wished to avenge the blemish he had put on him that day many years before when he, taking a young man of the Court with him, had gone bathing in a nearby lake called Loughrury. The river-horse, a monster who lived in the bottom of the lake, had seen them. Rearing itself up on its huge tail, it had thrust its serpent-like head out of the water, and opened its vast jaws to devour them in one gulp. Fergus had turned around and with powerful strokes made for the nearest bit of land as quickly as he could, permitting his attendant to swim before him so that he should not be in danger. Quickly in pursuit had come the monster, lashing the waters of the lake into a fury with its enormous tail, and breathing out of its mouth, as from a furnace, blasts of hot, foul breath, and sending a huge wave in front of it to break over their heads. Only just had Fergus and his companion gained the shore in time, but not before a blast of the monster's breath had reached the King, and so withered his face at one side that ever after his mouth was twisted around to his ear and his eye on that side squinted, and from that on he was known as Fergus Wryneck. But

Fergus had not known of this distortion, and the Queen, seeing him, had ordered that all mirrors be banished from the palace, and never was one to be left before him in any house where he might be on a visit. So for many years Fergus was not aware of his disfigurement, until one day a bonds-woman neglected to make his bath hot, and Fergus punished her by giving her a stroke of a switch he had in his hand, whereupon anger seized the bonds-woman and she cried out:

'It would become you more to avenge yourself on the river-horse that dragged your mouth around to your pole than to be hitting defenceless women.'

Fergus, hearing this, called for a mirror to be brought at once, and looking at his face he cried out:

'The bonds-woman's words are true. I am indeed a wrymouth.' And so it was that of all Iubadan's treasures Fergus desired the water-shoes.

Having got the shoes, Fergus now prepared to have his revenge on the river-horse. The day after he got them he rose early in the morning and set out for Loughrury. All the chiefs and nobles of Ulster assembled on the shore, some standing on the land and some in their galleys on the lake to watch the contest between King Fergus and the river-horse. Putting on the water-shoes, Fergus drew his sword and walked into the lake. The monster rose up and so lashed the lake with its tail that it began to look like a cauldron of boiling water, and all the boats that were on it were broken into matchwood, or filled with water till they sank to the bottom.

With sword held high and head erect, Fergus walked bravely up to the river-horse. Seeing him draw near, the monster opened its cave-like mouth and bared its teeth, its eyes blazing in its head like two great torches. Then, drawing back its ears, it lowered its snake-like head and made at him. Twice they fought the whole round of the lake, the monster beating up the water with its powerful tail and its thrice fifty flippers, each with a claw larger than that of a giant wildcat, until the foam and spume, thrown up on the hills, was like to a snowstorm in January. Then they sought the deep middle of the lake, and the watchers from the shore now saw the waters rise and fall like mountainous waves, and they saw that now the foam cast at their feet was red and gory.

At last from out the stormy, boiling waters they saw the head and shoulders of Fergus rise up. Standing erect, and with head held proudly on high, he waved his sword aloft in his right hand, while in his left he held up the horrible, gory head of the monster for all to see. Then as he stood the lake grew quiet about him, and all became silent as a summer's day. Speechless with love and pride, his people gazed on his pale and bloody face, and they saw it fair and comely as of old. And as all his people looked at him in love and silence, he raised aloft the monstrous head and shouted:

'Ulstermen, I have conquered.'

And gently his sword fell from his hand, and dying, he slipped down into the bosom of the lake.

# *IN THE TIME OF FINN AND THE FIANNA*

# I

# THE YOUNG FINN

MANY hundreds of years after the time when the famous Red Branch Knights lived in Ulster there lived another group of warriors in southern Ireland, and they in time became as famous as the Ulster heroes. They were called the Fianna of Erin. Like the warriors of the Red Branch, every man of the Fianna was a picked man, chosen for his strength and bravery, and specially trained in warfare and athletic feats so that he became a champion among warriors. This gallant band, under their own leader or chief, were bound by strict rules of chivalry, and were sworn to fight for the High King against any foreign foes who might invade the country, and also to keep the peace among the sub-kings or petty chiefs within the realm.

In times of peace the Fianna lived a free open-air life devoted to the chase, for they were great hunters as well as warriors. In summer time they lived altogether in the open, sleeping in sheilings or bothys made of reeds and saplings, and feeding themselves on whatever fell to their arms in the chase. And there was never any scarcity of food, for in those days Ireland was covered with vast forests, where the wild boar, the deer and the wolf roamed in plenty, and those the Fianna hunted with their famous dogs—the Irish wolf-hound, as large as a small pony and now, alas, almost extinct. In a single day's hunting it is said that they would go from Killarney, in Kerry, to Ben Eadar in the east, near where Dublin stands to-day, crossing the trackless bogs and forests and climbing the mountains' slippery sides, and the wet day and the fine day, winter or summer, were all the same to them, for they heeded not wet nor cold.

'I used to sleep out on the mountain-side under the grey dew,' said Oisin, the warrior poet of the Fianna. And of his father, Finn Mac Cool, he said:

'Finn's favourite sleep music was
The cackling of the wild ducks on the lake of the three Narrows,
The scolding of talk of the blackbird of Derrycairn,
The lowing of the cows from the Valley of the Thrushes.'

Finn Mac Cool was the greatest leader the Fianna ever had, for, as well as being a brave warrior, he was a wise and just man, and under him the Fianna rose to its highest fame. Finn's father, Cool, had been the head of the Fianna too, but in his day a rival clan, the Clan Morna, wishing to get the headship for one of their own family, rose in revolt against Cool, and fighting a bloody battle against him at Cnucha, near where Dublin stands to-day, slew him and drove his followers, the Clan Baiscne, into exile in Connacht, where, hiding in the lonely glens, they thought to escape the vengeance of Clan Morna. Goll Mac Morna then took the leadership of the Fianna and appointed new officers from among his own clan. From the dead hand of Cool he took the Treasure Bag of the Fianna, and gave it to Lia of Luachair, a chieftain of Connacht, for it was he who gave the first wound to Finn in the battle of Cnucha. So Lia of Luachair was made treasurer of the Fianna and keeper of the magic weapons that had been given to them by the gods, and the strange, wonderful things that had come from the Eastern World that had the power of healing wounds and sickness in them, and as well there were jewels and other wondrous gifts that had come out of the land of Faery.

After the routing of Cool's followers at the Battle of Cnucha, Muirna of the White Neck, the wife of Cool, went into hiding too, making south to Kerry with some women of her household. While traversing the wide Bog of Allen on her way to the south, Muirna gave birth to a son, whom she named Demna. As she looked down on the face of her newly-born boy, she saw in it again the face of Cool, her warrior husband, whose blood was still reddening the grass on the plain of the Liffey behind her. Quickly, for the rumble of Goll Mac Morna's chariot was rolling nearer through the forest, she put her son into the hands of her two bonds-women, and bade them take him to some remote place in the mountains and rear him in secret until he would be of an age to challenge Goll Mac Morna for the leadership of the Fianna. Then, saying farewell to her son, she went quickly on her way.

The two women, one a druidess and the other a wise woman, took Demna by secret paths into the Slieve Bloom Mountains in Tipperary, and there, in a lonely fold of the hills, they reared him in secret. As he grew up they trained him to hunt and to fish and to throw the spear, and he became so skilled with his weapons that he could bring down a bird on the wing with a single cast of his sling, and he was so swift a runner that he could overtake a stag on foot and could kill him with no one to help him. So Demna came to boyhood ranging the mountains and the bogs, with no companions but the pole-cat and the rabbits, the hare and the deer, so that he grew to love Nature and all the sounds and the sights of the wild mountains and the bogs, the rivers and the woods, and that love remained with him all during his life. After his death his son Oisin said of him that the things his father loved most were:

> 'The clamour of the hunt around the mountain steep
> The belling of stags in the rocky glen
> The screaming of gulls over the stormy sea
> And the sound of the torrent in valleys deep.

The song of the blackbird of Letterlee
The strong wave pounding the rocky shore
Tossing his boat on the plain of the sea
The talk of the grouse on the heathery slope.'

Now, as Demna grew older and stronger he became more adventurous and began to wander far from his home among the mountains. One day he reached the plain of the Liffey, and there he came on the house of a great chieftain. In a field near the stronghold he saw some boys of his own age playing hurling. They gave Demna a hurley and asked him to play with them. In the game that followed there was not one that could equal his speed in running, and very soon, as he learned the rules of the game, he could play as well as any, and even take the ball from the best on the field. Next day he played with them again, and though they put one fourth of their number against him, he won the game. The day after they put half their number against him, and he won that game too. On the fourth day all the twelve played against him, and Demna won the game from them all. That evening the chief of the stronghold, hearing of Demna's athletic skill, questioned the boys as to his appearance, and they told him that he was tall, shapely, and very fair. 'Then let us call him Finn,' said the chieftain, 'if he is as golden haired as you say', and from that on Demna became known to all as Finn.

Rumours of Finn's skill and daring now spread throughout the country, and at last they came to the ears of Goll Mac Morna. Goll listened to these tales with great unease—tales of the unknown fair-haired youth who with one cast of his spear could kill a bird on the wing, and could run down on foot the fleetest stag in the forest, and single-handed could win a game of hurling against twelve opponents. As he listened, Goll's thoughts went back to the day he had killed his enemy, Cool, on the green plain of the Liffey. He recalled Cool's wife, Muirna of the White Neck, and the rumour of the birth of a son in the forest as she fled before his trackers. He counted on his fingers. That son would now be fourteen years old—a dangerous young wolf-cub, sharpening his spears, measuring his spear-cast and practising his swordplay before challenging the slayer of his father. Clan Morna, Goll now knew, was in danger. Quickly he mustered his Fians around him and told them of Finn and of his deeds, and warned them to be on the lookout for him. Calling for his trackers he sent them out to the north and to the south, to the east and to the west to scour the mountains and the forests for any sign of this fair-haired youth, and to bring him back dead or alive.

In their remote dwelling, among the back hills of the Slieve Bloom Mountains, Finn's two foster-mothers, hearing of these trackers, called Finn to them and said to him:

'You must leave this place now, for the sons of Morna are coming to kill you, as they killed your father before you, for you and not Goll are the rightful leader of the Fianna of Erin.' So Finn, gathering together his hunting gear and buckling on his arms, took leave of his two foster-mothers and, as the old story-tellers say, 'took the world for his pillow'.

Finn now wandered around the country, taking military service with petty kings and chieftains, and so gaining in strength and skill of arms in preparation for the day when he should challenge Goll Mac Morna for the headship of the Fianna. But once, when in the service of the King of Kerry, Finn won seven games of chess, one after the other, from his master. The King, greatly surprised at his skill in the game, looked at him closely and said:

'Who are you, and of what people do you come?'

'I am the son of a peasant of the Luigne of Tara,' answered Finn.

'No,' said the King, 'you are not the son of a peasant. You are the son that Muirna bore to Cool. And you must not stay here any longer, for those that seek to kill you may be too powerful for me to protect you against them.'

And so it was everywhere Finn went, people suspected, either from the beauty and dignity of his person, or from his skill and knowledge in the hunt or in the contest, that he was no common youth travelling the country seeking his hire. The time seemed to have come for Finn to take the next step towards the goal that he had set himself—to gain the captaincy of the Fianna and to set up again his own family, the Clan Baiscne. So, gathering around him a band of youths who admired his strength and courage, Finn turned his face to Connacht to seek Crimnal and the remnant of Cool's followers who had been hiding there since Cool's defeat at Cnucha.

One day as Finn and his followers were going along through the country they came on a woman of noble bearing who was crying and lamenting over the body of a dead youth. As she looked up at Finn, who had asked the cause of her grief, tears of blood flowed from her eyes and she cried out:

'This is my only son, Glonda, and he has been slain by Lia of Luachair and his followers. I now put you under bonds as a warrior to avenge his death, since there is none other to avenge it.'

Finn took up the challenge, and seeking out Lia of Luachair killed him with his own hand. Now, Lia of Luachair had a strange bag with him, made of the skin of a crane and patterned in red and blue. Finn took the bag and opening it found a spearhead of blue steel, finely wrought and well-tempered, a helmet, a shield and a belt made of the skin of a pig, and many other things that neither Finn nor his companions could divine.

Finn took the bag and he and his followers went on their way west over the River Shannon. Not long were they travelling when they came to a rude dwelling in the woods, made of plaited branches and roofed over with reeds and osiers. As Finn and his companions stopped to examine the rough structure, out from their hiding-places came, one by one, a number of gaunt and bearded old men clad in ragged skins, and carrying old and rusty weapons in their skinny hands, for they thought that the Clan Morna had at last discovered their place of retreat, and they had decided to fight and die rather than surrender without a struggle. Some touch of noble dignity that still clung to the ragged band caused Finn to cry out on seeing them:

'You are the Clan Baiscne whom I seek this day. Which of you is Crimnal, brother of Cool?'

Hearing this, one of the ragged group stepped forward, and looking fearlessly at Finn and his followers he said aloud:

"I am Crimnal, brother of Cool.'

And Finn looked at him and he looked long and earnestly at Finn, and as they looked into each other's eyes they knew they were of the one blood and of the same clan. Silently Finn knelt before Crimnal and laid at his feet the strange bag he had taken from Lia of Luachair.

'The Treasure Bag of the Fianna,' said Crimnal; 'surely the time of our deliverance has come.'

Slowly he opened the bag and laid bare its priceless treasures one by one, and as his old comrades watched him, their eyes grew bright, their weapon-hands tightened on their spears and swords, and age seemed to drop from them instantly.

'This,' said Crimnal, turning to Finn, 'is the Treasure Bag of the Fianna that Goll Mac Morna took from Cool as he lay dead on the field of Cnucha. The old books say that with its recovery Clan Baiscne will again rule the Fianna. Go forth and prepare to take your rightful place, O Finn, son of Cool.'

When Finn heard this he took leave of Crimnal, and bidding farewell to his companions, he went off to study poetry and the telling of tales with a wise man called Finnegas, who lived on the River Boyne in the east of the country, for he knew that before he could become a member of the Fianna he had to understand the rules of poetry and to have by heart a number of the old tales.

Now, Finnegas the Bard had been living on the banks of the Boyne for seven years, seeking to catch the Salmon of Fec which lived in a still, dark pool in the shade of overhanging oak trees. The Salmon was the Salmon of Knowledge, and it had been prophesied that he who would eat of the Salmon would get all the wisdom of the world.

Finn had not been long studying under Finnegas when one day Finnegas at last caught the Salmon. Warning him not to eat even the smallest bit of it, Finnegas gave it to Finn to cook. Finn put the Salmon on the spit to roast, and when it was cooked he took it up and laid it before his master. Finnegas looked at Finn as he served him, and as he looked he thought he saw the light of wisdom and the fire of poetry shining in his eyes.

'Have you eaten of the Salmon?' asked Finnegas.

'No,' said Finn, 'but when I was turning it on the spit it burned my fingers, so I put my thumb into my mouth to ease the pain.'

'That's enough,' said Finnegas; 'you have eaten of the Salmon of Knowledge, and in you the prophecy is fulfilled.'

Then he gave Finn the Salmon to eat, and from that on Finn had the eternal knowledge that the Salmon got from eating the nuts of the nine hazel trees that grow beside the well at the bottom of the sea. Finn then made a poem to summer to show he was proficient in poetry.

'MAY-DAY

May-day! delightful day!
Bright colours play the vale along.
Now wakes at morning's slender ray
Wild and gay the blackbird's song.

Now comes the bird of dusty hue,
The loud cuckoo, the summer-lover;
Branchy trees are thick with leaves;
The bitter, evil time is over.

Swift horses gather nigh
Where half-dry the river goes;
Tufted heather clothes the height;
Weak and white the bogdown blows.

Corncrakes sing from eve to morn,
Deep in corn a strenuous bard!
Sings the virgin waterfall,
White and tall her one sweet word.

Loaded bees with puny power
Goodly flower-harvest win;
Cattle roam with muddy flanks;
Busy ants go out and in.

Through the wild harp of the wood
Making music roars the gale—
Now it settles without motion,
On the ocean sleeps the sail.

Men grow mighty in the May,
Proud and gay the maidens grow;
Fair is every wooded height;
Fair and bright the plain below.

A bright shaft has smit the streams,
With gold gleams the water-flag;
Leaps the fish and on the hills
Ardour thrills the leaping stag.

Loudly carols the lark on high,
Small and shy his tireless lay,
Singing in wildest, merriest mood,
Delicate-hued, delightful May.'

Then he left Finnegas and started out once more on his wanderings.

# II

## HOW FINN BECAME HEAD OF THE FIANNA

When Finn left Finnegas on the Boyne he wandered off over the country again, free as a bird on the wing or the fish in the trackless ocean, taking no thought of what he might do next, but awaiting whatever adventure might fall to him. Turning west, he came over the rolling grassy plains of Meath till he reached the road to Tara and to the north. There he saw great multitudes of horsemen, kings out of Munster and Leinster with their queens riding by in chariots, and chieftains out of far Cork and Kerry with their followers and household troops all bound for Tara to attend the Great Assembly that the High King held there every year at Samain time.

Up in Tara, the High King, Con of the Hundred Battles, sat in the Great House of the Mead-Circling and received his guests, placing each in keeping with his position and his birth. From all over Ireland they had come there, kings, chieftains and warriors, and deadly enemies sat down unarmed beside each other, and drank the royal mead and made merry without fear or anxiety, for it was a royal decree that for the six weeks of the Great Assembly no quarrel was to be remembered and no weapon was to be drawn.

At the high table sat the King, the sub-kings and the nobler chieftains, while below them, in the central portion of the hall, sat the High King's officers and the fighting men of the Fianna, with Goll Mac Morna, their leader. By the coming of dusk the hall was full, the torches flared from their sconces on the walls, and the wine-goblet and mead-cup had circled many times around the tables, when up the hall strode a tall, fair stripling. The youth made his way to the table where the officers of the Fianna sat, and laying aside his arms took a seat among their ranks. Every eye was on him as he seated himself, for to all there assembled this youth of the honey-coloured hair and the noble bearing was a stranger. The High King of Ireland looked at him no less than the others, and calling one of the wine-servers to him, bade him take a goblet of wine from the high table to the newcomer and ask his name. On receiving the wine Finn stood up, and in a loud, clear voice, that carried from one end of the Mead-Circling Hall to the other, he said:

'I am Finn, son of Cool, son of Trenor, who had, before the time he came to his death, the command of the Fianna of Erin. And I have come now to enter your service, O King, and to put my sword at your command.'

'Young man,' said the King, 'if you are the son of Cool you are the son of a friend, and the son of a trustworthy hero.'

And calling Finn to him, he bound him in service and loyalty to himself, and then he gave him a place at his own table, seating him side by side with his own son. Then the feasting and merriment went ahead as before.

Now, about this time, and for twenty years previous to it, a goblin called Aillen of the Flaming Breath used to come out of a fairy rath near Tara every Samain, during the Royal Assembly, and burn Tara to the ground. This goblin came by night, and as he came he played sweet music on a silver harp, and all who heard the fairy music fell into a deep sleep. Then, when all were in deep slumber, the goblin used to throw out of his mouth a blast of flame that burned

Tara till there was nothing left of it but a heap of black ashes. So as the hour approached midnight, and the torches began to burn low in their sconces on the wall, an uneasy murmur seemed to run along the high table between the High King and his guests. The warriors at the table of the Fianna too grew strangely silent, and looked fearfully at one another. Then the King stood up and said that he would give a mighty reward to any warrior who would keep Tara safe from the goblin's fiery breath till the break of day on the morrow.

The High King waited, but the warriors of Erin made no answer, for all knew that at the first sound of that plaintive fairy music even wounded men writhing in agony of pain would fall asleep.

Finn, having listened to the King's words, thought in his own mind that this was his chance to prove his valour, and to show his worthiness to become a member of the Fianna. He stood up, and turning towards the King said in a loud and steady voice:

'If I, Finn Mac Cool, kill the goblin and save Tara for evermore, will you bind yourself, O King, before all the kings of Erin here present, that I will get my rightful heritage—the captaincy of the Fianna of Erin as a reward?'

And Con answered:

'I bind myself to what you ask, and the kings and princes of Erin and Kithro the Magician will be my sureties on it.'

Then Finn got up, and taking his weapons went out of the banqueting hall to pace the ramparts of Tara, and to keep it safe from the Goblin of the Flaming Breath.

Among the King's household troops at this time was one Fiacha, who had been befriended by Finn's father in his youth. Now, when Fiacha saw the youthful Finn leave the hall and go out alone to fight the goblin he followed him, and as Finn paced the ramparts on his lonely watch Fiacha drew near and handing him a spear, whispered in his ear:

'This is a spear of enchantment that will help you in the dangerous task you have taken on yourself.'

Finn took the spear and unlaced its leathern wrappings, and as he looked at the blue steel blade and its thirty rivets of Arabian gold they winked and shone in the moonlight like the stars above his head in the frosty November sky.

'Take it,' said Fiacha. 'It was fashioned by Len, the swordmaker to the gods who used to work in Loch Lene. He beat into it the heat of the sun and the light of the moon and the stars. When you hear the fairy melody from sweet stringed tympan or silver harp place its cold, blue blade against your brow and no sleep shall overcome you.'

Finn took the spear and began to pace the ramparts once more, and as he went he looked across the wide, grassy plains of Meath that lay white with frost under the November moon, and as he looked he strained his ear for the first notes of Aillen's fairy music. Not long had he to wait, for scarcely had he made another half-circuit than he heard it, far away on the plain, the first wisp-like sounds from sweet strings, gentle and soft as the dawn breeze, rising and falling like the sighing of a summer sea. Nearer and nearer it came as he stopped and listened enraptured, forgetful of everything except the music that was now gently enfolding him like a vapour. Then, floating across the white moonlit fields, he saw Aillen, wraith-like as the moon itself, and playing the tympan as he came. At the sight of the goblin Finn roused himself from his torpor and with all the power that he could muster, for the fairy music had begun to weave its spell around him, he unloosed the spearhead from its case, and with his two hands quickly pressed the cold blue steel against his forehead.

On came Aillen, sending out before him a long tongue of flame, but as he approached him Finn ripped off his fringed saffron mantle and cast it on the flame, quenching it to the ground. Seeing this, the goblin turned and fled back across the plain to the fairy rath from whence he had come, but Finn, following quickly behind him, was just in time to cast Fiacha's magic spear after him as he glided in the door. The spear went through the goblin's breast and felled him to the ground at the door of the rath, and Finn, drawing his sword, beheaded him, and putting the head up on the point of Fiacha's spear set it up on the ramparts for all to see.

When day had dawned, and Tara being still untouched by the fiery breath of Aillen, the King and all the warriors of Ireland knew that Finn must have overcome the goblin, so they came out on to the ramparts to see for themselves. The King now standing with Finn at his right hand spoke to the Fianna of Erin:

'Warriors of Erin, you have heard me pledge my word that I should give the headship of the Fianna to this warrior if he should but save Tara from the burning raids of Aillen. He has killed Aillen, and he is now your leader by every right that men of bravery and men of their word hold to. Those who will not obey him, let them leave.'

And turning to Goll Mac Morna the High King said:

'What is your choice, Goll, son of Morna? Will you quit Erin, or will you lay your hand in Finn's?'

And Goll Mac Morna answered:

'I pledge my word that I will lay my hand in Finn's.'

And there in the presence of the High King and all the Fianna, Goll swore a bond of fealty to Finn Mac Cool, and after him each warrior swore obedience and loyalty to their new leader, and so it was that Finn Mac Cool became head of the Fianna.

# III

## FINN AND THE FIANNA

It was under the leadership of Finn that the Fianna rose to the height of their glory and became renowned through the land for their valour and bravery, for Finn, as well as being a great warrior, was a born leader. He was beloved by all the Fianna, even by his former enemies the Clan Morna, because he was just and generous. Of his justice it used to be said that if he had to decide a quarrel between his enemy and his own son he would be as fair in his judgement to one as to the other. Of his generosity, the old story-tellers used to say: 'If the leaves falling from the trees in autumn were gold, or the white foam on the waves silver, Finn would give it all away.' Of his bravery there can be no doubt, for he was the greatest fighting man of his day, and the only one to compare with him in bravery was his grandson Oscar, who, according to the old story-tellers, became the bravest of all the Fianna. So each Fian followed the example set them by Finn, and each put his honour and the honour of the Fianna above his life, or, as Goll Mac Morna, one of the most famous of them, said:

'A man lives after his life, but not after his honour.'

So highly did Finn rate his Fians that to become a member of the Fianna in his day was considered a high honour, for no one was admitted unless he could pass a number of severe tests. First he had to show that he was skilful and dexterous as well as brave. To prove this he had to stand in a deep hole in the ground and defend himself with a shield and a hazel rod from nine men casting spears at him. If he got as much as a single scratch he was not taken. Then they fastened his hair in braids and a number of the Fianna chased him through the woods. If he were overtaken or wounded he was not chosen, or if his spear trembled in his hand, or a strand of his hair became undone, or if a dry stick cracked under his foot as he ran. After that he had to leap over a branch the height of himself, and run under another one level with his knee, and while running his fastest he should be able to pick a thorn out of the sole of his foot without slackening his speed.

Then before he was admitted he had to know the twelve books of poetry and to recite from them, and also he had to have a number of the old tales by heart. When all these tests were passed he was bound by Finn to four pledges: not to take a dowry with a wife, not to take cattle by force of arms, never to refuse help to any man with cattle or riches, and never to fall back before less than nine fighting men.

The best fighter and the bravest man that Finn had under him was the old enemy of his tribe, Goll Mac Morna. Finn in a poem praising Goll said that Goll was brave in battle, and though as strong as the wave pounding the shore, and as hardy and as fierce as a hound, he was kind and gentle to his friends.

Keelta Mac Ronan, another of the Fianna, was famous for his speed as a runner; it was he that, single-handed, ran down and killed the enchanted boar whom the Fianna had been hunting for many years without as much as touching one hair of his hide. Another time Keelta overtook and killed a five-headed giant who had been taking cattle and sheep from every farmer in Erin. Keelta is said to have lived longer than any other of the Fianna, except Oisin, who was away with the Faery for three hundred years, and he was alive at the time Saint Patrick came to Ireland with news of the one true God.

Dermot of the Love-spot was another famous warrior of the Fianna. Dermot was tall and handsome, and it was said of him that no woman could look upon his face without falling in love with him.

The bravest of all the Fianna was Oscar, the grandson of Finn, and the old tales say that Finn wept only twice in his long life, and once was at the death of Oscar in the Battle of Gowra.

Finn and the chief men of the Fianna lived with his household in Finn's dun on the Hill of Allen in the present County Kildare. And though to-day there is no stone left of Finn's palace on the heather-covered hill, the ramparts and the ring forts are still there to be seen, and there are people living close by who will tell you that on many a moonlit night they have seen Bran and Sgeolaun, Finn's two favourite hounds, loping through the heather and whining with impatience like dogs that have been kept too long waiting for the chase.

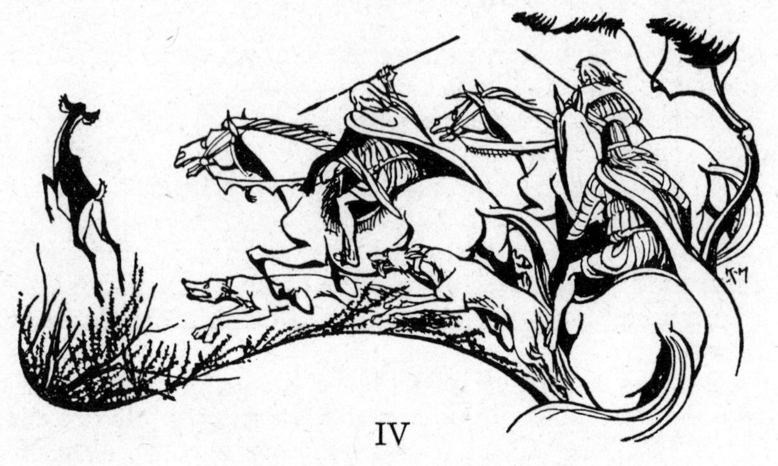

# IV

## THE MOTHER OF OISIN

ONE evening on their way home from the hunt Finn and his followers were riding back to Finn's dun on the Hill of Allen in County Kildare when a beautiful fawn started up out of the heather in front of them. The whole party gave chase for a while, but as it was the end of the day and men and dogs were tired they soon fell back, all except Finn with his two dogs, Bran and Sgeolaun, who kept up the hunt. After some time Finn began to catch up with the fawn, and was nearly upon her when suddenly, to his great surprise, he saw her lie down in the heather in front of him. Bran and Sgeolaun now began to frolic around the fawn, making gentle friendly noises and licking her head and body. Up she got then and ran along towards the Dun of Allen with the two dogs, who placed her in between them, as if for protection. Arriving at the palace, she followed them into the great hall, and lay with them at Finn's feet, while Goll Mac Morna, Keelta and Dermot O Dyna supped with him at the great table over their heads.

That night as Finn lay in bed he suddenly saw appear at his bedside the most beautiful maiden that his eyes ever rested on. She spoke to Finn and told him who she was, and as she spoke her voice was like the sound of summer waterfalls, or the gentle May-time breeze playing in the tree-tops of a young wood.

'I am the fawn you chased this evening, O Finn,' she said. 'My name is Sava, and I am a maiden of Faery, but the Black Druid of the Faery Folk has changed me into a fawn because I would not agree to be his wife.

'For three years now have I lived as a deer in the woods and wild places of Erin, being chased by cruel dogs through the length and breadth of the country. But a serving-man of the Black Druid told me that if I once gained the palace of Finn, on the Hill of Allen, my enchanter would have no more power over me. All day have I been making my way to your dun, O Finn, and never once have I stopped until I gained its heathery slopes and met Bran and Sgeolaun. I knew I was safe with them, for they have human wits, and they knew I was enchanted like themselves.'

Finn then spoke gently to the maiden, and told her to have no fear:

'Stay in Allen as long as you wish, and you will have my protection and the protection of the Fianna, and the Black Druid will have no power to harm you.'

So Sava stayed in the Dun of Allen and Finn fell in love with her, and made her his wife. So great was Finn's love for Sava that he gave up hunting and all other sports that would take him away from Allen and her, and so they lived in great content and happiness for many months.

But one day news came to Finn that sea-robbers had come in their ships to the bay where Dublin stands to-day, and were robbing and pillaging all before them. So Finn called together the seven battalions of the Fianna, and prepared to march against the Men of Lochlann and drive them out of Erin.

Then Finn and his men set off to fight the invaders, but before he went he took a tender farewell of Sava, and entreated her to keep well within the ramparts of the dun during his absence:

'I go from thee, Sava, not for the hunt, or the contest, but to fight the enemies of Erin, and to drive them out of the land. Guard thyself well while I am away, and in a short time we shall be together again. And I charge thee to keep within the ramparts of the dun, and hold no converse with anyone not of our household.'

For seven days Finn and the Fianna fought against the Northmen, killing many and driving off the rest, and at the end of that time he turned south for the Dun of Allen and home. On his march southwards over the plain of the Liffey, and over the flat Kildare bogland, Finn thought only of Sava, and of the joy of their coming meeting, and of the great welcome she would have for him. Then as they drew near the heathery slopes of the Hill of Allen, and saw his great, gleaming white dun crowning the hill-top, he strained his eye for the first glimpse of his beloved wife, who doubtless would be waiting and watching for him on some high tower or window. But Sava was not on the rampart, nor on any window nor look-out that Finn could see. And when he reached his dun he saw that the servants looked at him strangely, and there seemed trouble and anxiety in the eyes of all.

'Where is the fair lady of Allen, that she comes not to the rampart to meet me?' asked Finn.

'Alas, O Finn,' they made answer, 'while you were away fighting, one day a man with your very look and shape on him, and with two dogs of the very likeness of Bran and Sgeolaun, came up the hillside towards the dun. And Sava, who ever watched the plain for your return, saw them and rushed to the gates, and heeding not our counsel to stay within, dashed down the hill toward the phantom. Then, as we looked, we saw her stop before she reached it and utter three sad and bitter cries. She tried then to turn back, but the shadow raised a druidical wand over her head, and Sava became a fawn, and slipped away through the heather. Up the hill she ran toward the gate of the dun that was now wide open, but the hounds were after her, and before she could gain the gate one sprang at her throat and brought her down. Then a great baying of hounds and a rushing sound of feet and horsebeats filled the air, so seizing our arms we hurried down the hill and followed the sounds of horses and hurrying feet for many miles over the plain. But nothing could we see, and very soon the sounds too died away, and then there was neither sight nor sound of fawn nor dog nor druid.'

Finn listened to this story without a word, and then went silently to his own chamber. There all alone he sorrowed that day and for two days after, eating no food and speaking to none. Then, on the third day, he came forth from his chamber once again to look to the affairs of his household and of the Fianna.

After this he went out searching the country, and for seven years he was going up and down the land, and there was not a hill nor a hollow, a glen or a forest that he did not go through to see if he could find any sign of the fawn that Sava had become. And the only dogs he would take with him were Bran and Sgeolaun, for he knew that the gentle fawn would be safe with them.

At the end of the seven years' search, when Finn had given up all hope of ever finding Sava, he took up hunting once more. One day, when he and some of the captains of the Fianna were chasing over the shoulder of Ben Gulban, the hounds suddenly began to whine in a strange unearthly way, and running into a fold among the rocks, where they had gathered together, Finn and his men saw them in a circle around a beautiful young boy with long golden hair. Not a whit afraid, the boy stood at the mouth of a cave looking at the hounds. Bran and Sgeolaun licked and frolicked around him and kept the other hounds off from coming too close. When Finn and his captains spoke to him the boy looked from one to the other of them with a steady, undaunted look, but not one word could he answer to any of the questions they put to him. They took him to their hunting-booth, where he shared their evening meal, and then they took him back with them to the Dun of Allen.

After some months the boy learned to speak, and little by little lost all his wildness, and in a short time he was able to tell Finn the story of his mother and of his birth which Finn was anxious to hear; for as he looked into the gay, bright eyes of the boy, and marked his features, it seemed to Finn that he had a look of Sava—his lost Flower of Allen. And the story the boy told was that he had known neither father nor mother except a fawn who had always lived with him in the lonely, rocky valley where they had found him. He slept at night in the cave, except in the warm weather, when his bed was in the heather or on the sun-warmed rocks. He ate roots or fruit in the summer, but in the winter warm food used to be left for him in the cave near his bed. The only man he ever saw was a dark, angry-looking one who sometimes came to the valley and spoke to the fawn. Sometimes he spoke to her in a loud, angry voice, and sometimes he was soft and gentle, but no matter what way he spoke to her the fawn always drew away from him in fear. The last time the dark man came to the valley he spoke for half a day with the fawn, at first very gently and softly, but when the fawn drew away and would not listen, the dark one took out a hazel rod and struck her with it. Then quietly and sadly she turned and followed him out of the valley, but all the time she kept looking back at the boy with sad and tearful eyes, until at last, weeping bitterly, she went from his sight behind a rock. When he tried to get up and follow her, he had not the power to move a limb. Then when at last he could not see the fawn any longer he fell on his face on the grass, and his senses left him with grief. When he came to himself he was on another hillside—the one where the dogs had found him—and though he had searched every day for the hidden valley where he had lived with the fawn, he could never find it.

As Finn listened to the boy's story he looked into his face, and when he had finished he said to him:

'You will be my son and live with me always, and the name that will be on you is Oisin.'

And from that day on Oisin lived with Finn, his father, in the Dun of Allen, and became one of the bravest champions of the Fianna as well as their poet and story-teller.

# V

## THE PURSUIT OF DERMOT AND GRANIA

GRANIA was the daughter of Cormac, son of Art, High King of Ireland, and no woman in the length and breadth of the country could compare with her in beauty and grace. Many princes and chieftains sought her hand in marriage, but Grania was proud and she spurned each one after the other.

At this time Manissa, wife to Finn Mac Cool, died, and Finn, complaining to some of the Fianna of his loneliness, 'with no wife to cheer or comfort me', was advised by them to ask Cormac for his daughter, Grania, in marriage. Finn agreed, and Oisin his son, and Dering O'Bascna, a warrior of the Fianna, set out for Tara to take Finn's request to the High King.

When they reached Tara, the King was holding an assembly of his chiefs and nobles, but hearing of the coming of Finn's messengers he put off the assembly until next day, in order to welcome them and to hear their business. But when Oisin told the King that they had come to ask for Grania as a wife for Finn Mac Cool, he told them that they should go and tell Grania of Finn's request and get her answer for themselves. 'For,' he said, 'there is hardly in all Ireland a king or a son of a king that has not asked for

Grania in marriage, and she has refused them all, and this has made many an enemy for me throughout the land.'

So Oisin and Dering went to the apartments of the women, that were at the sunny side of the palace, and Cormac, going with them, said to his daughter:

'Here, Grania, are two warriors of the Fianna whom Finn Mac Cool has sent to ask you to be his wife.'

And Grania answered, with as much thought as if it was a lap dog or a pet bird she was being offered:

'If you think he is a worthy son-in-law for you, why shouldn't he be a suitable husband for me?'

Oisin and Dering were satisfied with Grania's answer, and they set out for Allen bearing a message from the King to Finn that he should come and claim his bride at the end of two weeks. So the warriors returned and told Finn how they fared, and gave him the King's message. Finn then collected around him the captains of the seven battalions of the Fianna to be his bodyguard, and he set out for Tara when the fortnight was up. The King received them with great honour and welcomed them to a feast in the great banqueting hall, and he bade all the nobles and chiefs of the province to come and make merry with them. Finn sat at the high table with the Queen and Grania and other royal persons, while Oisin and Finn's bodyguard sat at a special table set aside for the warriors of the Fianna.

While the feast went on Grania spoke with Dara of the Poems, who sat near her, and said:

'Tell me, Dara, what means all this feasting and merry-making? And why has Finn come to Tara with all his captains?'

And Dara, knowing not what to answer, said:

'If thou dost not know, it is indeed hard for me to know what has brought them hither.'

Again Grania asked the same question, and as she was hot-tempered and wayward Dara thought best to answer her, saying:

'Surely thou knowest that he has come to claim thee for his wife.'

Hearing this, Grania was silent for a while, and then she said: 'It would be no cause to wonder if Finn should seek me as a wife for his son Oisin, or even for his grandson, Oscar, but I wonder greatly that he asks me for himself, since he is a man as old as my own father.'

Then her eye wandered over the famous warriors of Finn's bodyguard as they sat at the table of the Fianna, and again she spoke to Dara of the Poems:

'Tell me, O Dara, who this noble company is, for I know none among them but Oisin and his son, Oscar. Tell me, who is the warrior on the right of Oisin?'

'That noble-looking warrior,' said Dara, 'is Goll Mac Morna, the Fierce in Battle.'

'And who is the graceful, slim warrior next to him?' she questioned.

'That,' said Dara, 'is the swiftest runner of all the Fianna, Keelta Mac Ronan. And the handsome warrior next to Keelta, with the grey shining eyes and the raven-black curls, is Dermot of the Shining Face, the most beloved of women, the most chivalrous and generous of all the warriors of Finn.'

Grania now began to sip her wine from her wine-cup and for a while she held no more converse with Dara, but all the time her eyes were wandering to Finn, and from him to his warriors at the lower table. Then, as the talk became louder and the merriment had reached its height, she beckoned her serving-maid to her, and whispered in her ear:

'Bring me the large jewel-studded drinking-cup that holds wine for nine times nine men.'

The serving-maid brought the drinking-cup, and Grania, filling it with enchanted wine, gave it to her and bade her bring the cup to Finn:

'And bid him drink it and say it is Grania who sends it to him.'

Finn took the cup and drank a long draught from it and then handed it to the King, who, having drunk, passed it to the Queen, and to all at the high table. Very soon all those who had drunk from Grania's cup fell into a deep slumber.

Grania now rose up and, going to Dermot, said to him: 'Will you take my love, Dermot, and take me away from this house to-night?'

'I will not take you from this house,' said Dermot, 'for you are promised to Finn, and I will not meddle with any woman that is betrothed to Finn.'

And then Grania said:

'I put you under bonds, O Dermot, and bonds that no true heroes ever break, to take me out of Tara to-night, and to save me from this marriage with an old man.'

'Those are evil bonds, O Grania, and nothing but evil and strife can come of them.'

And then Dermot pleaded with her to withdraw her bonds and to give her love to Finn, as she had promised, 'For Finn is nobler and more deserving of a maiden's love than any man of the Fianna.'

But Grania would not listen, and then Dermot said:

'Dost thou not know that when Finn sleeps at Tara he keeps by his right and due the keys of the great gates, so that even if we wished it we could not leave Tara?'

'There is a secret wicket-gate in my bower,' said Grania.

'It is not fitting for an honourable warrior to leave a man's house by a wicket-gate,' said Dermot, still trying to put off Grania.

But Grania would not be put off so easily, and she reminded Dermot that any Fian would easily jump over the palisades by using his spear as a jumping-pole.

Greatly troubled in his mind between Grania's bonds under which she bound him as a warrior sworn to help all women in distress, and his loyalty to Finn as his leader and his friend, Dermot asked the advice of Oisin, Oscar and Keelta as to what course he should take. But they all urged him to keep the bonds that Grania had laid on him to help her.

Dermot stood up then, and, stretching out his hands for his weapons, sadly bade farewell to each one of his Fenian comrades. And as he clasped their hands he wept, for he knew that never again would he be their comrade in war or in peace, in the ale-feast, or in the chase, as long as he lived, for to go away with Grania was to go out of the Fianna for ever, as he knew that the vengeance of Finn would pursue him to the end of his days.

Then, turning to Grania, he said:

'It is a hard journey you are drawing on yourself, O Grania, for there is no corner of Ireland that Finn will not search for you and for me. But I will go with you, though it is not my wife you will ever be, for I will keep faith with Finn.'

'I will not draw back now, Dermot, and I will never part with you till death itself comes between us.'

And they took to the trackless wastes of Ireland, and fled before Finn, and their house was the glenside and the lonely forest, and the sky over their heads was their only roof, and their pillow the sod under their feet for the long years that stretched in front of them. And all over Ireland, in summer and in winter, Finn pursued them with his hirelings, for the Fianna would take no part in Finn's quarrel with Dermot. And so closely did he follow them that in whatever place they cooked their food they did not stop to eat it, and in whatever place they ate it they did not stay to sleep, and in whatever place they lay down to rest at the coming of night they did not rise up there on the morrow.

One day when they had got tired of travelling they came to a thick wood known as the Wood of the Two Huts. Here Dermot put up a bothy of saplings and osiers wherein they might rest. All around the outside of the hut he raised a palisade of strong larch-poles that no man could knock down, and he put seven narrow doors in it, each facing seven different parts of the wood. But Clann Nevin, the trackers that Finn had for running down Dermot and Grania, came on the palisade, and climbing up into a tall tree they saw Grania inside. This news they took back to Finn, and he came to the wood, bringing along with him some of the Fianna and some of his hirelings.

Finn placed his men at each of the seven doors of the palisade and then called on Dermot to come out. When Grania saw that they were surrounded by Finn's men great fear seized her and she began to cry. But Angus of the Birds, the god of Love and Beauty and the foster-father of Dermot, seeing the plight of his foster-son, came to their help, passing unseen over the palisade.

'Let each of you come under the border of my cloak,' said he to Dermot, 'and we will pass out unseen by Finn and his people.'

But Dermot asked him to take Grania away to a safe place, and he himself would fight his way out, as became a warrior. And Grania did as Dermot said, and she and Angus went off to the Headland of the Two Swallows, and there they waited for Dermot.

Dermot then drew himself up as straight as a pillar, and taking his arms he went to one of the doors and asked who was there, and the answer he got was:

'No enemy of yours but Oisin and Oscar. Come out by this door and no one will touch a hair of your head.'

But Dermot said:

'I will not go out by this door, for I do not wish to bring the anger of Finn down on you for letting me go free.'

Then he went to the next door and asked who was keeping watch there.

'Keelta Mac Ronan with Clann Ronan around him. Come out here and we will fight for you to the death,' was the answer he got.

'I will not go out by this door,' answered Dermot, 'for Finn would rather see you all dead than that I should escape him.'

And so it was with all the doors up to the sixth, and at that door Finn stood guard himself, and this was the door that Dermot sought to go out, for he did not wish to bring Finn's anger on any of the Fianna who wished to let him go free. So standing before the sixth door Dermot shouted:

'I will pass out through this door, Finn, the door that you are keeping yourself.'

Dermot then, using the staves of his spears as jumping-poles, rose with a light, high leap and cleared the palisade and went out over the heads of Finn and his hirelings, and far beyond them. Before they saw where he landed, Dermot had got away, and turning towards the south, made for the Headland of the Two Swallows. There in a woodland hut he found Angus and Grania waiting for him, and they had a wild boar on a spit of hazel, roasting before a blazing fire. When she saw Dermot, Grania's heart leaped within her with joy. Then he told them all that had befallen him, and they ate a hearty meal and slept peacefully that night, and when the morning light was lighting up the world they arose.

Then Angus of the Birds took leave of his foster-son, saying:

'I am going away from you now, O Dermot my Son, and before I go I want to leave this advice with you. Do not go into a tree with one trunk when flying before Finn: never enter a cave that has only one opening; and never land on an island that has only one harbour; and where you cook your food there eat it not; and where you eat, sleep not there; and where you sleep to-night, sleep not there to-morrow night.'

Then Angus bade them farewell, and they went on their way. And for a long time they remembered the advice of Angus, and did not sleep two nights in the same place, and they travelled up and down the country, sleeping at night under dolmens or out in the heather if the night were fine. But once more they got tired of travelling and they longed to stay quietly for a while in one place that would be safe from Finn and his trackers.

One day, many months after parting with Angus, they came to a dense, thick forest—the Forest of Duvros in the west of the country. In this forest there was a magic quicken tree that was guarded by a fierce, ugly giant known as Sharvan the Surly.

'We will stay here in this wood,' said Dermot, 'for this is the only place in all Ireland where Finn will not follow us.

The Fianna never hunt here, and no trackers of Finn will dare enter the wood, for fear of the dreadful Surly.'

Dermot then went off and left Grania resting at the edge of the forest while he made an agreement with Surly the Giant. He got leave from the giant to stay in the wood and to hunt there for his food, but he swore on his sword that never would he come near the magic quicken tree or touch one of its berries. Then he came back to Grania and made a fine sheiling for her with oak wattles and boughs, and Grania was happy, for their wandering was at an end for a while to come.

Now, some time after this Finn and the Fianna were hunting in a part of the country half a day's journey away, when his trackers came and told him that Dermot and Grania were in the Wood of Duvros. He knew that the wood was guarded by Sharvan the Surly, and that neither he nor his trackers could follow them there, so he sent for two of the sons of Morna, with whom he had a feud, and whom he knew would be well pleased to obtain his pardon and be brought into the ranks of the Fianna.

The sons of Morna came at his bidding, and he told them that he would make peace with them and give them places in the Fianna if they would undertake a task for him.

And the sons of Morna, glad to think that their long feud with Finn was over at last, answered:

'Name your price, O Finn, and we will do your bidding.'

'The price of my friendship is the head of a single champion or a fistful of berries,' said Finn.

'The head of Dermot, grandson of Duivne, is the head he is asking of you,' said Oisin, who was listening, 'and if you were a hundred men in their full strength, Dermot would not let you take that head.'

'And what are the berries he is wanting?' asked the sons of Morna.

'There is nothing harder to get than those berries,' said Oisin, 'for they are the fairy berries growing on the magic quicken tree in the Wood of Duvros, and this is how they came to be there.

'It happened one time that a dispute arose between two women of the Faery people, Aoife and Aine, as to which of their men was the better hurler. Aoife was married to one of Finn's captains, and Aine was married to one of her own people—the people of the Faery. So Aoife and Aine agreed that the men of Faery should challenge the men of the Fianna to a hurling match, and so as to make out which were the better hurlers, it was to be played near Loch Lene.

'The match was settled for a certain day, and all the people of Faery came hither from their own land, bringing provisions and food for their people, and the food that they had were crimson nuts, and apples and sweet-smelling, juicy rowan berries. And as they were passing by Duvros Wood one berry of the rowan berries they had fell from them and a tree grew up out of it. And the berries that grew on that tree were bigger and juicier than any rowan berries anyone ever saw, and anyone that would eat one of them would feel them to be as lively as wine, and as satisfying as old mead. And if there was any sickness on him it would go with the eating of a single berry, and any old person would become young again, and if a young girl ate them she would become as beautiful as a flower.

'When the people of Faery found out that a magic quicken tree had grown up in Duvros Wood, they put a guard over it, for they did not wish that mortals should eat of fairy food and become themselves immortal. And the guard they put over it was a terrible giant, with long, crooked tusks, and having only one eye in the centre of his forehead, and no weapon could kill him, only three strokes from his own iron club, and that club he never left out of his hands, sleeping or waking.

'And now,' said Oisin, 'is it any cause for wonder that the Fianna never hunted in that wood?

'So it is against Sharvan the Surly you must go,' said Oisin to the sons of Morna, 'if you want to get a fistful of the berries of the magic quicken tree for Finn. And I warn you that it would be no avail for you to go against him, for no mortal champion can overcome him.'

When the sons of Morna heard this they spoke a little while apart with one another, and then they said to Finn:

'We will do what you say, for we cannot go back now, and we would prefer to come to our deaths seeking the berries for you than to have it be said we were afraid of Sharvan the Surly.'

And so they took leave of Finn and set out for the Wood of Duvros.

Next morning they came to the edge of the forest, and finding the track leading to Dermot's bothy they followed it. Dermot heard them coming, and, jumping to his feet, put his hand out for his weapons and went out to face them. He asked them who they were and what brought them to the Forest of Duvros.

They told him that they were the sons of Morna, who had been at war with Finn ever since the Battle of Cnucha, and that Finn had now agreed to make peace with them and had given them the choice of two tasks: either to get Dermot's head, or a fistful of the berries from the magic quicken tree.

'It is no easy matter for you to get either of those two things,' said Dermot, 'but choose now, O Children of Morna, between combat with me for my head, and getting the berries in spite of Surly.'

'I swear by the blood of my people,' said each of the sons of Morna in turn, 'that I would sooner fight with you for your head.'

So they got ready for a wrestling bout with Dermot, and he wrestled with each one after the other, and in a short time he threw them in turn, and then he bound them hand and foot.

'Tell me,' said Grania, who had been listening to the talk between Dermot and the sons of Morna, 'what are those berries that Finn has such a wish for and that are so hard to get?'

Dermot then told her the story of the magic quicken tree, and of the berries that grew on it that made the old young and the young beautiful, and were as heady as old wine and as satisfying as old mead.

'By my word,' said Grania, when she heard all this, 'I will not be content ever again until I taste some of those berries, and no food will I take from this on till I taste them first.'

'Do not make me break my agreement with Surly,' said Dermot, 'for he will never let me take those berries without a fight.'

But Grania insisted that she wished to taste the berries and that she would refuse all other food until she had tasted them. So Dermot got his arms together and prepared to go against Surly. And very loath he was to do so, for he knew that from this on once again they would have no shelter over their head but the wide sky, for it was fear of Surly that kept Finn from following them into the Forest of Duvros.

The sons of Morna, hearing Grania's request, asked Dermot to unloose them from their bonds and they would go and get the berries for her. But Dermot would not agree to do this, and he said:

'I will go myself, for if you were but to get one look at that monster you would most likely die on the spot with fear and terror.'

Then they begged Dermot to unloose their bonds so that they might go and see the combat between himself and the giant, and this Dermot agreed to do.

When Dermot and the sons of Morna drew near the magic quicken tree they found the giant asleep, and Dermot shaking him by the shoulder to awaken him said:

'I come, O Sharvan, to get a fistful of berries from your faery quicken, for Grania, Daughter of the High King of Ireland, wishes to taste them and I am now asking your leave to take them to her.'

Sharvan the Surly jumped up when he heard this, and taking his club swung it over his shoulder and shouted out in rage and fury:

'I give you my word that if Grania or the High King of

Ireland himself were to die for want of those berries they will never taste one of them.'

And so saying he rushed at Dermot and brought his club down heavily on him, but Dermot leaped aside and the giant's iron club dug its spiked head harmlessly into the ground. Then, catching Surly off his guard for an instant, Dermot leaped at him and tore the great club from his hands, and raising it over his head with a mighty effort struck three strong blows on the head of the giant and felled him to the ground. Then the sons of Morna came and buried the body of Surly so that Grania should not see it. And they went and brought Grania to Dermot so that she should taste the berries of the magic quicken tree.

When Grania came back with the sons of Morna, Dermot went up the tree and picked a handful of berries for them, and they sat down and ate their fill of them, and soon all the weariness of the combat with Surly passed from Dermot and he felt in his full vigour again. Then the sons of Morna picked a fistful to take back to Finn, and Dermot and Grania climbed up into the tree where Surly had had his bed, and there they concealed themselves in the thick branches, for Dermot knew that now that the giant had been killed Finn would not make any delay in coming after them.

When Finn got the berries from the sons of Morna the first thing he did was to smell them, and as he held them under his nose he called out:

'I swear that it was Dermot, son of Duivne, that picked those berries, for the smell of his skin is on them, and I am sure it is he, too, that has made an end of Surly the Giant, and I will go now and find out for myself whether he is living or dead.'

So mustering his hirelings and his men of the Fianna he set out for the Wood of Duvros, and reaching it he followed the track that lead him to the magic quicken tree. By this the great heat of the day was making Finn drowsy, so sitting down under the shade of the great wide-spreading tree, he told his followers that he would rest there till the cool of the evening. 'For,' he said, 'I know that Dermot is on top of the tree.'

And Oisin, who was listening to him, said:

'There is no doubt at all that your brain is clouded by

jealousy to say that you believe that Dermot would wait for you at the very place that you would be most certain to seek him.'

But Finn made no answer, but called for a chess-board to while away the time. He began to play with Oisin, and Oscar and Dering looked on, sitting by the side of Oisin to advise him. Finn played a very cunning and skilful game against all three, and at last there was only one move Oisin could make, and Finn said to him:

'There is but one move now that would give you the game, Oisin, and I defy you and those advising you to know what that move is.'

And Dermot, who was watching the game through the branches of the tree, threw a berry down on the man that should be moved. Oisin moved that man and won the game from Finn.

Then Finn began another game with Oisin and brought him to the same pass as before where one move, if he but knew it, would win the game for him. Again Dermot threw down a berry on the man that Oisin should move, and again Oisin won the game from Finn.

Then they played a third game, and the same thing happened.

Then Finn said:

'I do not wonder that you won the three games, Oisin, when you had the skill of Oscar, the watchfulness of Dering and the prompting of Dermot, son of Duivne, to help you.'

'That is a great sign of jealousy in you, Finn,' said Oisin, 'to think that Dermot would stay up in that tree all this time when he knows that you are on the look-out to kill him.'

'With which of us is the truth, Dermot?' Finn shouted up the tree.

'Your judgement was always sound, Finn,' said Dermot, 'for it is true that Grania and I are here over your head in the place of Surly the Giant.' And then Dermot gave three kisses to Grania in the sight of Finn.

'You will pay with your head for those kisses,' said Finn, and he called his hirelings to him, and bade them surround the tree, promising them that whatever man would take Dermot would have his arms and his armour and a place among the Fianna as a reward.

Then Garva of Slieve Cua stepped forward, saying that it was Dermot who had killed his father and that he was glad of this chance to avenge him, and he began to climb the tree.

Now it was made known to Angus of the Birds that Dermot and Grania were in danger again, and once more he came to their help. When Garva of Slieve Cua was climbing the tree Dermot sent him reeling backwards with the force of a mighty kick, and as he fell to the ground Angus put the shape and appearance of Dermot on him, so that Finn's men cut off his head, but as he died his own shape came back on him again, and then Finn knew that Dermot was still alive.

Then Garva of Slieve Crot said, 'It was Dermot's father, Donn, that slew my father; and I will now avenge him on Dermot.' So he climbed the tree. Again Dermot hurled him back, and as he fell to the ground Angus put the shape of Dermot on him again, and again Finn's men cut off his head.

And so it went on till all the nine Garvas had been killed, and Finn was full of anger and sorely puzzled at seeing this.

Then Angus of the Birds said he would take Grania to a place of safety. And Dermot said:

'Take her and watch over her tenderly. If I live I will follow you, and should I not live take her to her father in Tara, and tell him to use her well.'

So Angus of the Birds wrapped his magic cloak around Grania, and unseen by Finn and his men they passed out over their heads and made for the Brugh of Angus at the Boyne.

Speaking down to Finn now, Dermot said:

'I will go down to you now, O Finn, and I will deal out slaughter all around me on you and on your men. For certain it is that you have made up your mind to make an end of me and to give me no rest. And I have no refuge against your hatred, for I have made enemies for myself in Erin and throughout the wide world fighting for you, for you were never in any war or trouble that I did not go into for the sake of my love for you and for the Fianna.'

'Dermot is but speaking the truth, O Finn,' said Oscar, Finn's grandson. 'Give him peace and pardon now.'

'I will not do that,' said Finn, 'to the end of life and time.'

Then Oscar, answering Finn, said:

'I give you my word as a champion, O Finn, that unless the skies fall on top of me or the earth under my feet open and swallow me, I will not let any man of your men touch a hair of Dermot's head. And I now take him under my protection against all the men of Ireland.'

Then Dermot stood up on a high branch of the tree, and

using the shaft of his spear as a jumping-pole rose with a great leap out over the head of all those below him. And Oscar made towards him, and together they cut their way through those of Finn's hirelings that tried to stop them. They went on to the Boyne then, where Dermot found Grania in the safe keeping of Angus of the Birds.

And Dermot lived for a while on the Boyne with Angus and Grania until in the end Angus went to Finn and asked him to make peace with Dermot. And Finn said he was willing, and the High King of Ireland also pardoned Dermot and gave Grania her dowry of land, the cantred of Kesh-Corran in Sligo. And Dermot got back his lands and held them without rent or tribute to the King of Erin, and he got a guarantee from Finn that the Fianna would not enter them or hunt over them without Dermot's leave. Then Dermot and Grania went to live in that portion of their lands in the county of Kerry, farthest from Finn and Cormac Mac Airt, and there they built themselves a house called Rath Grania, in which they lived in great peace for many years. And Grania bore Dermot four sons and one daughter, and it was said that there was not a man in Ireland at that time who was richer in silver and in gold, in cattle or in sheep, than was Dermot son of Duivne.

# VI

## OISIN IN THE LAND OF THE EVER YOUNG

ONE morning in the early summer Finn and the Fianna were hunting in the woods around Loch Lene near Killarney. Mists covered the glens and were draped around the tops of the mountains, but soon the rising sun shot diamond spears down through the clouds, and turned the lakes into twinkling jewels in the dark bed of the glen. Waiting for the mists to clear, Finn and his companions sat on a hillside, but Oisin, his son, stood gazing down on the lakes and rivulets of silver, for Oisin was the poet of the Fianna and he loved the beauty of the lakes, the bogs and the mountains, and the creatures of the forest and the sea. Now he called to his comrades to look at the sun lighting up one misty valley and lake and rivulet after the other, and he reminded them that it was here, in these jewelled and shining ravines, hundreds of years before their time, that Len the mighty smithy and armourer to the gods of Erin had his anvil. And it was here he beat out the magic spears and swords and javelins for Lugh of the Long Arm, and for Nuada of the Silver Hand, for Manannan Mac Lir, the sea-god, and for all the warriors of the People of Dana. And so much magic did he beat into them that, like the famous spear of Lugh, they had to be kept steeping in a pot of poppy-seeds to soothe them and keep them quiet, so thirsty were they for blood. As Len worked he made around him sparkling rainbows and fiery dews that falling to the ground made the lakes and silver streams, and the sun-shot mist that ever since plays around Loch Lene.

The Fians looked down on the lakes beneath them as Oisin was telling them of Len, and as they looked they saw a small cloud of mist come out of the valley, and waft up the hill towards where they sat. When it drew near it broke in two and out from it stepped a milk-white steed and a rider clad in scarlet and gold.

''Tis Len himself who rides towards us,' said Finn.

But as the steed came nearer, the Fianna saw that its rider was not Len, but a maiden of great beauty, and she was clad in the raiment of a queen. On her head she wore a crown of gold, and the bridle in her hand was studded with glittering jewels. Her steed was shod with shoes of pure gold, and silver bells adorned his harness of white bronze and red leather. Pulling up the steed, the maiden spoke to Finn, and said:

'Finn son of Cool, I am Niav of the Golden Hair, daughter of the King of the Land of the Ever Young, and I have crossed the seas for love of your son Oisin, the poet and music-maker of the Fianna.'

Then she looked at Oisin and asked him if he would return with her to the Land of the Ever Young. And in a voice like a gentle summer breeze playing over silver bells, she sang to him of the beauties of her father's kingdom.

'Delightful is the land beyond all dreams!
    Beyond what seems to thee most fair—
    Rich fruits abound the bright year round
    And flowers are found of hues most rare.

Unfailing there the honey and wine
    And draughts divine of mead there be,
    No ache nor ailing night or day—
    Death or decay thou ne'er shalt see!

The mirthful feast and joyous play
And music's sway all blest, benign—
Silver untold and store of gold
Undreamt by the old shall all be thine!

A hundred swords of steel refined,
A hundred cloaks of kind full rare,
A hundred steeds of proudest breed,
A hundred hounds—thy meed when there!

A hundred maidens young and fair
Of blithesome air shall tend on thee.
Of form most meet, as fairies fleet,
And of song more sweet than the wild thrush free!'

As they listened to the maiden's song, the Fianna stood stock still, as men under a spell, so bewitched were they with her beauty and with her sweet-sounding voice. And while she sang no bird called out, nor bee was heard to buzz, nor stream to murmur, but over all a silence and a stillness seemed to steal, until the song was ended. Then, finishing her lay, she raised a lily-white arm and waved Oisin to a seat by her side on the white steed.

Gently, like one in a dream, Oisin moved towards her, and mounting the fairy steed he sat by the side of Niav of the Golden Hair. And as the steed wheeled around to go, Oisin for a moment rested his dream-laden eyes on Finn, who was calling out in anguish to see him leave. Then as they galloped off down the hill he looked back once and waved a languid arm in farewell.

They went like the wind over bog and mountain, and soon Oisin could no longer hear the wails and lamentations of his comrades. Then they came to the rocky coast of Kerry, and the fairy steed pranced lightly over the crests of the waves and made out to sea. As they passed over the sun-dazzled floor of the ocean they seemed to enter a land of golden light and pearly dew, a land of rainbow and sunshine, where on either side of them, as they went, they saw rise up the tall pinnacles of mansions and castles shimmering and shining over lawns of softest green and banks of brilliant flowers. Over their heads, embosomed in the clouds, were cities of marble and gold, that seemed to disappear before a second glance. Once a yellow fawn chased by a pure white hound with one red ear went by, and then a beautiful maiden riding on a bay, and holding a golden apple in her hand. After them again they saw a young knight in flowing purple cloak, and in his hand a flashing sword of gold, riding past them mounted on a pure white steed.

Oisin wondered at all these strange and wonderful sights, but Niav bade not to notice these visions, as there was nothing of real beauty to be seen until they reached the Land of the Ever Young.

Then they left the region of sun and brightness, and now dark thunder-clouds rolled over them; and daggers of rain and arrows of lightning shot around their heads. But they rode on through the tempest, going as quickly as leaves before the wind, until at last they left the storm behind them. Now they saw a land of great splendour rise up before them out of the sun-kissed ocean.

Their steed faced for this sunny land, and soon was riding up over a silvery strand and on to lawns of sweet-smelling clover shaded by giant beech trees, where the song of many birds mingled with the hum and buzz of a myriad bees. Here Oisin saw the people leave their houses and come out to welcome him and Niav, some on foot and others riding steeds as richly caparisoned as their own, and all were young and beautiful and gay.

'What lovely land is this?' asked Oisin of Niav.

For answer Niav smiled and led Oisin through a noble gateway into a palace bawn, where a hundred riders on black steeds, and a hundred on white were drawn up for their reception. Out from the rows of horsemen rode the King of the Land of the Ever Young, and in a loud voice, so all could hear, he welcomed them to his kingdom:

'Welcome, Oisin son of Finn! Welcome to this land where we honour poets, where there is neither age nor sorrow nor death. Where time does not wither away, and every day brings only joy! Take Niav for thy bride, live with us for ever, and speak poems of love, of life, of beauty and of joy, and of youth that never grows old!'

Then the King of the Land of the Ever Young led Oisin into his palace and presented him to the Queen. And that day Oisin was wedded to Niav, and he sat beside her at the royal banquet that was made in honour of their wedding. There he ate off plates of purest gold, while minstrels played strangely soothing strains on harps of silver, and men of poetry sang joyous and lovely songs, and all the while from the open casements blossom-fragrant winds played around their heads, and brought to their ears the song of birds from the deep, cool woods.

So from one delight to another day followed day till Oisin knew not whether he lived in one long lovely dream where bliss was unending. He had only to wish for something and it came to pass, and all the delights of his old life with the Fianna, the hunt, the ale-feast, the horse-races and the sports, he savoured over again—only now they were always more perfect, more delightful and more joyful than those of his mortal home.

But at night in his dreams Oisin visited Erin again, and once more took up his old life with his Fenian comrades, hunting the deer or the wild boar in the great forests of the south, fishing in the great lakes and waterfalls of the Shannon, or horse-racing in the great plain of Kildare. Then with the power of longing for his old life he would awaken from his sleep, and stride up and down his chamber in strange unease and still half asleep. But before his full waking came to him Niav, ever watchful of his happiness, would be by his side to read his wish and to bring back his content.

'I thought to be chasing over Ben Eader's heathery side after the fleetest deer that ever ran, and Finn was by my side, and Keelta Mac Ronan and Dermot of the Beautiful Women, and Finn's dogs, Bran, Sgeolaun and Lomair . . .' he would tell her.

And Niav, seeing the longing and sadness in his dream-laden eyes, would quickly order the horses and dogs to be got ready, and before Oisin could have time for one other regretful thought, he would be riding down a woodland avenue on his black steed, on his way to the hunt with Niav and other joyous youths and maidens. And as the woods rang with the winding of the hunting-horn, the pounding of a hundred hoof-beats, the belling of stags and the musical clamouring of hounds, Oisin's dream and longing would melt away and be banished for ever from his mind.

But one day Oisin, riding away from Niav and his companions in the hunt, found himself on the border of a bleak and desolate land. And as he stood and looked around him, trying to discover his way back to the hounds, he thought he heard the sound of the Dord Fianna, Finn's hunting-horn, faintly echoing away among distant hills in the bleak land before him. He listened again, and as he heard the faint sound, once more his dreams of hunting with the Fianna came back to his mind. Closing his eyes he saw the sun-warmed, honey-fragrant heather on which they lay—Finn, Dermot, Keelta, Conan the Bald and Goll son of Morna—and at Finn's feet stretched out, with loving eye and lolling tongue, his favourite hounds, Bran and Sgeolaun. Now all the forest had gone still around him and only the bees in the tree-tops made a sound. Slowly Oisin turned his horse's head towards the dim hills in the bleak land before him, and with eager desire he pressed on and on, to where he still fancied he heard the dim echo of the Fianna's horn.

Soon he reached a region of bare rock and trackless boggy mountain, up which his steed scrambled with fear and reluctance. Gone now were all sight of leafy summer woods, and lawns of sweet-smelling clover. Up and up horse and rider pressed until they reached a land where steely icicles clung to the black rocks, and drifts of snow hid chasm and miry, dangerous places before them. Inky thunder-clouds pressed down around them, while the wind shrieked with horrible, demon-like fury. Up and up over an ever-steep icy mountain they went, the steed clinging with clever hooves to the slippery and dangerous rocks, till at last, high among the mists and clouds, they reached a dreary, foggy plain. And here, among floating drifts of the wind's icy breath, there loomed an ugly black fortress, ancient and battle-scarred.

Oisin dismounted, and drawing his sword he walked towards the great iron-studded door. At the side of the door he saw a deep cave, and in its dark depths a maiden of the fairest face he had ever seen, and she was chained to two ancient eagles. As he drew near, the maiden called out to Oisin to beware, and dragging on her rusty chains she came to the mouth of the cave and spoke to him.

She told him that the castle he saw before him was the castle of the Fomor, a monster and a giant of such strength that no champion in the world could conquer him, for she said he was 'as strong as a mountain, as crafty as the fitful winds, and as lasting as the salt sea that eats away the world'. She told him, too, that she had been imprisoned here for so long that she had lost count of the centuries, and that many bold warriors had come from the eastern and the western worlds to rescue her, but all had been made an end of by the Fomor. He was so evil and so frightful, she told him, that he put the demons screaming and jabbering at night, with fear of him, and these were demons that he had put in prison for growing lax in their evil-doing.

'Go while you may from this evil and horrible place,' she begged of him, 'for there is no chance that you will not be put to death by the Fomor.' And while she spoke her rusty chains clanged around her, and the old eagles winked their steel-sharp eyes.

For answer Oisin strode up to the mighty door of the castle and with his sword struck three heavy blows that resounded down the dark and vasty corridors, causing a chorus of shrieks and inhuman horrible wails from the captive demons in the deep dungeons within.

Slowly the rusty door groaned open, and a horrible monster of evil countenance came out fully clad for battle, carrying shield and sword and a giant iron-spiked club.

With a roar like the rolling of thunder between high mountains he rushed at Oisin, and swinging his great club over his head he thought to bring it down on Oisin's skull and shatter it to pieces. But Oisin leaped nimbly out of the way, and before the slow-witted and cumbrous Fomor had recovered from his surprise at his opponent's swiftness, Oisin leaped on him and thrust his sword deep into his breast. Forth gushed a spout of blackish-brown blood as Oisin withdrew his blade from the Fomor's chest, and now that the first blood was spilt the fight became fierce and quick. The Fomor rushed at Oisin, and his iron club danced around his head and body with such speed that no eye could see where it was going to fall. So Oisin closed with the giant, and for many bouts blows were given and received that could not be counted. Then at last the Fomor gave a mighty blow with his club that glanced off Oisin's head and crashed on his shield with a stunning and thunderous noise. Oisin staggered, but recovered himself quickly, and turning on the giant, who thought to have felled him, drove his sword right through his shoulder and sent him reeling to the ground.

Out from the shadows servitors of the Fomor now rushed to bear their master away to safety, and to apply healing oils and unguents to his many wounds. From the shadows, too, came Niav, gliding to the side of Oisin, and together they withdrew into the cave where the maiden was chained to the two ancient eagles. As he lay on a pallet of otter-skins, Niav, with healing oils and sweet-smelling balm distilled from rose-petals and water-lilies, soothed and healed his many gashes and wounds, and gently chiding him for leaving the Land of the Ever Young, she put a restful slumber on him, and he slept for many hours. But as the first ray of the dawn crept in through the mouth of the cave he leaped to his feet once more and got ready to fight the Fomor. The Fomor, too, healed by magic oils and balms, arose strong and ready to renew the struggle.

And so for seven days they fought, and at the end of each day no one could say whether Oisin or the Fomor was the

victor. But each evening as Oisin came back to have his wounds healed, and to seek restful slumber in the cave, he saw that one chain less was binding the beautiful captor to her eagle jailers. Then at the end of seven days, when he put forth all his strength, Oisin leaped at his enemy in an unguarded moment and ran his sword right through his heart. Down sank the giant, and as his life-blood ebbed away in a murky stream across the castle yard the last of the rusty chains that bound her to the ancient eagles dropped from the waist of the beautiful maiden, and she was free, and with much rejoicing she went out towards Oisin and led him in to his rest and healing. Then taking a steed from the Fomor's stables she left for her own land and her own people, whom she had not seen for many hundred years.

Then, too, Niav and Oisin mounted their steeds, and with a speed that outraced the wind they left the dark region of the Fomor for ever, and turned their faces towards that land of gladness and joy—the Land of the Ever Young. As they passed over the confines of that cold shadowland of the Fomor they came to a great dim lake that, deep in moss-quiet woods, stretched out to far unknown shores. As they passed by its leaf-hidden waters Niav urged on her steed more quickly, but something drew Oisin's eye to where the driftwood bobbed on the dark ripple by the stony shore, and caused him to start and pull up his racing steed. Quickly dismounting, he went to the edge of the water, and there picked out from among the floating leaves and straws a spear-shaft washed up from mortal shores, a spear-shaft made of the wood of the ash, such a one as the Fianna used to have.

For a long time Oisin stood by the lake-shore and gazed at the broken shaft, and never spoke a word to Niav, who now stood questioning by his side. For, as he looked, he saw the hand that had fashioned it, and the woodland by the side of Allen's heathery slopes where it had grown. Then he looked around him at the woods by the lake shore that now were fragrant with bluebell and white hawthorn—the flowers of May-time. And he thought: 'In Erin now the Fianna will be putting out long fishing-lines, for the mayfly are hanging in murmurous haze over stream and river, and the shining trout will be leaping, and the splash of the salmon will be making bright the dim forest pools.'

Then he said to Niav that he would return to Erin for a short visit to see Finn and the Fianna once again, and to tell them of his life in the Land of the Ever Young. But Niav grew sorrowful at the thought of Oisin leaving her for the land of the mortals, where, she said, the leaf dies on the bough, and the songbirds are silenced by winter's chilly blast, and the young and the beautiful are withered by age.

But Oisin answered that if the leaf dies, and the birds are muted by winter's cold, their coming with the spring is all the more beautiful when hope is born anew, and if the young and the beautiful grow old, they grow, too, in wisdom. And then he pleaded with her to give him leave to go.

'Let me go, if only for one short day in Erin, that I may grasp the hand of Finn and Dermot and Oscar once again, and tell them my story of the Land of the Ever Young, and then I shall return to your side and dwell with you for ever in your blissful country.'

And Niav answered:

'Go, Oisin, since you so desire to see your land and your people once again, but I warn you most earnestly not to dismount from your steed, or let your foot once touch the soil of Erin, or you shall never again see the Land of the Ever Young.'

So Oisin mounted his horse and faced for the land of Erin. It was on a May morning just as when he left that he returned again to his own country. The sun was breaking out through the light summer clouds when he felt the soil of Erin under his horse's hooves. As they rode along, Oisin's eyes eagerly scanned the hills and the valleys for any sign of the Fianna, and he strained his ears for the sound of their hunting-horn. But no sign or sound of the

Fianna could he see or hear, and on his journey through the land he passed by many strange new buildings, high and strong and built of stone, and from their towers a sound like that of great cymbals floated out over the country-side. He watched some churls building one such tower, and, as he watched them, great was his surprise at their smallness. And the churls greatly wondered at the giant size of Oisin and at the richness of his attire, and seeing him pass they laid aside the mallets and leaned on their spades, and called out to their fellows to come and see 'one of the gods of old that now again visits the earth'.

Then Oisin asked them if they knew in what part of Erin Finn and the Fianna were hunting at the present time. And one among them, who was in command—a druid, as it appeared to Oisin from his robes and his shaven head—called out that he should well know that Finn and his Fianna had gone from the world these three hundred years. But Oisin took him for a jealous, power-grasping druid, and spurred on his steed to Finn's chief dun on the Hill of Allen.

On through the broad oak forests in the middle of the country he sped, and never drew rein till he reached the side of the heathery Hill of Allen, rising out of the great bog around Kildare. Here it was that Finn's great household was, in the high dun on the hilltop, its lime-white mansions gleaming in the sun and plainly seen from many leagues away. But now the floating May morning mist obscured it from Oisin's view, or so he thought until he came out of the oak wood and climbed the hill, and then no mist or cloud was hiding the ruin of rath and hall, or the riotous nettles and elders and docks that covered the ramparts and banqueting hall of that once great dwelling.

Oisin pulled up his steed and looked wonderingly around him. No sound broke the awesome silence of desolation.

'No enemy that put his hand to this would live to finish it so fully, for Finn would have him killed before he had half begun,' thought Oisin.

Could it be that Finn has left Allen and built himself a larger dun nearer Tara? he mused.

Or could it be . . . and he remembered the words that the churlish druid had called out to him—that Finn and the Fianna had come to their end.

Frenzy seized Oisin at this thought, and, quickly turning his steed, he faced northwards to Tara of the Kings to seek news of Finn and the Fianna from the High King himself.

His way lay by the mountains that skirt the eastern sea, and as he went by the Valley of the Thrushes he saw a band of churls on the hillside toiling and sweating in the efforts to lift a slab of granite out of a quarry. Greatly marvelling at the sad change that had come over the race of men since his day in Erin—'Even the slaves were twice their size and four times their strength,' he thought to himself as he watched them—full of pity for their weakness he stretched out his arm, and, stooping across them, lifted the slab right out of the rock face.

The churls gazed at him with wonder and admiration, and sent up a shout of praise for the strength of the beautiful god that, they believed, had come among them. But the next minute their cheering changed to cries of terror as they fled in confusion at what they now beheld. For, in bending over to lift the slab, Oisin had broken his saddle-girth and had fallen to the ground. The minute he touched the ground the noble and powerful young warrior changed into a miserably aged old man, whose beard and hair were thin and white, and his arms, which he now stretched out for help, were as bony and fleshless as a skeleton's. Gone, too, was the royal purple mantle and the gold-bordered red silk tunic, and as for his steed with the golden hooves and the gem-studded trappings—all that was left of that was a white wisp of mist floating away over the brow of the hill.

Oisin had now become a mortal once more, and could never again return to the Land of the Ever Young. And the weight of three hundred years fell on him as he lay, and thinking of his wondrous life with Niav and with the Fianna of old the life went out of him, and he sank to the ground.

'An old man stirs the fire to a blaze
In the house of a child, of a friend, of a brother.
He has over-lingered his welcome; the days,
Grown-desolate, whisper and sigh to each other;
He hears the storm in the chimney above,
And bends to the fire and shakes with the cold,
While his heart still dreams of battle and love
And the cry of the hounds on the hills of old.'

# *TALES FOR THE CHIMNEY-CORNER*

The four folk-tales—The Black Thief, The Three Sons of the King of Antua, The Bird of the Golden Land and Finn Mac Cool, the Giants and the Small Men—are retellings of the versions taken down from Irish-speaking story-tellers in Kerry by Jeremiah Curtin towards the end of the last century.

*Beside the Fire*

Where glows the Irish hearth with peat
There lives a subtle spell—
The faint blue smoke, the gentle heat,
The moorland odours tell

Of white roads winding by the edge
Of bare, untamed land,
Where dry stone wall or ragged hedge
Runs wide on either hand

To cottage lights that lure you in
From rainy western skies;
And by the friendly glow within
Of simple talk and wise,

And tales of magic, love or arms
From days when princes met,
To listen to the lay that charms
The Connacht peasant yet.

There honour shines through passions dire,
There beauty blends with mirth—
With hearts, ye never did aspire
Wholly for things of earth!

Cold, cold this thousand years—yet still
On many a time-stained page
Your pride, your truth, your dauntless will
Burn on from age to age.

And still around the fires of peat
Live on the ancient days;
There still do living lips repeat
The old and deathless lays.

And when the wavering wreaths ascend
Blue in the evening air,
The soul of Ireland seems to bend
Above her children there.

*T. W. Rolleston*

# I

# THE BLACK THIEF

## I

## *King Conal's Horses*

LONG ago in Erin there was a King, and he was married to a Queen who was beautiful and kind. So kind was she that she was beloved by all the people of the land, especially the poor who came daily to the palace looking for help. Now this King and Queen had three fine sons, and they were the happiest family in Erin until the day the Queen took sick with a strange disease. Knowing she was going to die, the Queen called the King to her bedside and said to him:

'If I die and you marry again, promise me you will send my three sons away to a distant part of the kingdom, so that they may not be under the control of a strange woman, until they come to manhood.'

The King gave her his word that he would carry out her wishes and then the Queen died peacefully. The King mourned her sadly for a year or two, and never thought of taking another wife, until his councillors told him he should marry again for the good of the realm. He ordered a castle then to be built in a far distant part of his kingdom, and there he sent his three sons with servants and teachers to look after them. Then he married again and was happy once more until his new wife had a son.

One day, shortly after the birth of his new son, the King was out hunting, and the Queen went for a walk around the castle grounds. As she passed by the cottage of a half-crazy old hen-wife she heard the old woman complaining of her neglect of the poor, and shouting out after her as she passed by:

'It is little you care for the poor and the needy who live by your grand castle walls, not like the fine generous Queen your husband had before you. It was she was the grand lady that would take the cloak off of her own back and give it to them that wanted it more.'

Hearing her, the young Queen stopped to ask about the dead Queen, and promising the old woman a hundred speckled goats, a hundred sheep and a hundred cows to tell her all, she heard from her of the three sons the King had in the distant castle on the far side of his kingdom. 'And,' said the old woman, 'when they come of age your son will not have a place to lay his head, no more than the birds of the air.'

As she listened to the old hen-wife the young Queen began to sorrow for the fate of her son, but the old woman comforted her:

'Listen to me and I will tell you how to get rid of the King's three sons. Get the King to bring them back to the castle for a visit, and while they are there, challenge each one of them, one after the other, to a game of chess. I will give you an enchanted board to play on that will make you win. When you have won from the three of them, tell them that you put as a sentence on them that they should go for the three steeds of King Conal, and bring them back to you, as you want to ride three times around the boundaries of the kingdom. They will go, and you will never see them again, for many is the champion that went seeking King

Conal's horses and never came back again. Then your own son will be king when the time comes.'

The Queen went home, and that very evening when the King rode back from the hunt she asked him about his sons, and why he kept them away from her.

'Bring them back home,' she begged him, 'and you will see that I will be as fond of them as I am of my own son.'

So the King brought his three sons home, and had a great feast prepared to welcome them, and all the people of the country were delighted to see them back once more.

After the feast the Queen challenged each brother one after the other to a game of chess. She played three games with each one, she won two from each, and pretended to lose the third. That night the eldest son came to her and said: 'What sentence will you put on me and my brothers for having lost to you?'

'I put you and your two brothers under bonds not to sleep twice in the same house, or eat twice at the same table till you bring me the three steeds of King Conal, as I want to ride three times around the boundaries of the kingdom.'

'Where, O Queen, will we find the horses of King Conal?' asked the eldest brother.

'There are four quarters in the world,' said the Queen, 'and you will surely find him in one of them.'

'I will give you your sentence now,' said the eldest brother, 'for the game that you lost to us. I put you under bonds of enchantment to stand on the top of the castle, and stay there without coming down, and watch for us till we come back with the horses.'

'Remove from me your sentence; I will remove mine,' said the Queen.

'If a young man is relieved of the first sentence that is put on him he will never do any good,' said the King's son. 'We will go for the horses.'

Next day the three brothers said farewell to their father and set out to find the castle of King Conal. After travelling for many days and getting no tidings of the place they were seeking, they came up with a lame man who was wearing a black cap on his head.

'Who are you, what brought you to these parts, and where are you bound for?' asked the man of the black cap as he stood in front of them.

'We are the three sons of the King of Erin,' said the eldest of the three brothers, 'and we are looking for the three horses of King Conal to bring back to our stepmother.'

'Come and spend the night with me,' said the lame stranger, 'and to-morrow I will go with you and be your guide to King Conal's castle.'

So as dusk was falling the three brothers went with the stranger, and passed the night in his house. Next morning the man in the black cap called them early, and told them that trying to get King Conal's horses was a thing that had cost many a brave champion his life. 'But,' he said, 'I will help you, and maybe we will succeed, though without my help you would have no chance at all.'

So the four of them set out once more, and before nightfall they reached the castle of King Conal. They waited until the middle of the night before they went to the stables for the horses, and then great was their joy to find that all the guards were sound asleep.

The three brothers and the man with the black cap seized their chance and took a horse each and began to mount, but as soon as they touched them the horses reared up madly and began to neigh and whinny so loudly that they woke up the whole castle. The guards rushed on the three brothers and seized them at once with the man in the black cap and brought them before King Conal.

King Conal sat on a massive throne of gold in the great hall of the castle. At each side of him and all around the back of his throne stood his guards with drawn swords. In front of him was a great cauldron of oil boiling and bubbling over a blazing fire.

'Ah,' said King Conal, when he saw the man in the black cap in front of him, 'only that the Black Thief is dead, I'd say you were he.'

'I am the Black Thief,' said the man in the black cap.

'Indeed,' said the King, 'we'll soon find that out. And who are these three young men?'

'We are the three sons of the King of Erin,' said the brothers.

'Now,' said King Conal, 'we'll begin on the youngest. But stir up the fire there under the cauldron, for the oil is gone off the boil.'

Then the King turned to the Black Thief and said:

'Now, isn't that young man very near death this minute?'

'I was nearer death once,' said the Black Thief, 'and I escaped.'

'Tell me the story,' said King Conal, 'and if it's a thing that you were nearer death than he is this minute, I will let him go with his life.'

'That's a bargain,' said the Black Thief, and he began to tell King Conal the story.

II

# *The Three Enchanted Maidens*

'WHEN I was a young man I had lands and riches in plenty, and I lived in ease and comfort until three witches came and destroyed my property. Then I took to the roads and became a famous thief, the most famous that ever lived in Erin, the Black Thief.

'Now, these three witches were three daughters of a king that was in Erin at that time, and they were three of the most beautiful maidens in Erin during the daytime, but at night, because of a spell a wizard put on them, they changed into three hideous hags.

'Now it happened, before I lost my property and took to the roads, that I had my men cut and bring in for me a supply of turf to last me seven years. The great reek was raised outside my house, and it was so big that it looked like a black mountain. Well, late one night—after midnight it was—I was coming home from a banquet, and what did I see but the three ugly witches taking the turf from my reek and loading it into three creels on their backs and making off with it. That winter they never stopped taking it until they made off with every bit of turf I had.

'The next season I laid in enough turf again to last me

for seven years, but the witches came once more and took it off with them. Then one night I watched while they filled their creels, and I followed them into the hills, and there I saw them go down into an underground passage in the rocks, twenty fathoms deep in the ground.

'I looked down, and there I saw them below with a whole bullock in a pot and they boiling it over a great fire. I glanced around me for something to throw at them, and seeing a huge boulder near the mouth of the hole I heaved it and rolled it over till it crashed down on them below. It broke their pot and spilled their broth into the ashes of the fire.

'I took to my heels then, but soon the three witches were close behind me. I climbed a high tree to escape them, but they saw me and stopped underneath to look up at me through the branches. The eldest of the three hags then turned the second hag into a sharp axe, and the third into a fierce swift hound. Then, taking the axe, she began to cut down the tree underneath me.

'With the first blow of the axe the witch cut the tree-trunk a third of the way across. She gave a second blow and cut another third of it. Then she raised the axe for the third and last blow, but just at that moment a cock crowed, and before my eyes the axe turned into a beautiful maiden, the hag, who was felling the tree, into another beautiful maiden, and the fierce swift hound into a third. Then joining hands the three sisters walked away, as happy and innocent-looking as any three young maidens in Erin.

'Now,' said the Black Thief to King Conal, 'wasn't I nearer death that time than this young man is now?'

'Indeed you were,' said the King, 'but we'll have his brother instead of him. The oil is on the boil now; so there's no need to delay.'

'Even so,' said the Black Thief, 'I was once nearer death than he is this minute.'

'Let us hear the story of it,' said King Conal, 'and if you were, we will let him go with his life too.'

The Black Thief then began his second story.

III

# *The Thirteen Enchanted Cats*

'AFTER I had broken the pot of the three witches that had stolen my turf and my cattle, they killed all my hens, and trampled my crops, and left me so poor that I had to take to the roads as a thief to make a living for my wife and family.

'One night I was driving an old horse and cow home to feed my children when I got so tired from walking behind them that I had to sit down under a tree in a thick wood to rest myself. It was cold, and as I had a flint in my pocket I lit a bit of a fire to keep the heat in me. I wasn't long sitting by the fire when I saw, stealing around me out of the darkness, thirteen of the biggest and fiercest-looking cats that ever was seen within the walls of the world. Twelve of them were each the size of a fully grown man, but the thirteenth, their leader, was the size of any two of them put together. He was a great, powerful cat with fiery green eyes that shone and sparkled as he sat in front of the fire facing me. The others sat six at each side of him, and they began to purr all together, making a noise like thunder in the still night air.

'After a while the big red one raised up his head and looked across the fire at me and said:

'"I won't be hungry any longer; give me something to eat at once."

'"I have nothing to give you, unless you take that old white horse tethered to the tree over there behind you."

'The red cat made a spring at the horse and, making two halves of him, ate one half himself, and left the other to his twelve comrades. They tore it to pieces and picked every bone clean.

'Then the thirteen of them came back to the fire again, and sat around me licking their lips and purring with a noise like thunder. After a while the big cat spoke again and said:

'"I'm hungry again; give me some more to eat."

'"I have nothing to give you, unless you take the cow without horns," I answered.

'The red cat made for the cow and made two halves of her, as he did with the horse. One half he ate himself, and the other he left to his twelve comrades. While the fierce cats were eating the cow, I took off my coat, wrapped it around a log, and put my cap on top of it to make it look like myself, for I knew what they would do next. Then I quickly climbed the tree overhead.

'Soon the cats had finished every scrap of the old cow and they came back and sat around the fire once more. Then looking at the block of wood that I had put in place of myself, the red cat spoke again:

'"Have you any more food for me, for I am starving this minute?"

'The block of wood gave no answer, so the leader of the cats sprang across the fire at it and began to bite and tear it with his claws. But he soon found out his mistake.

'"Aha," he said, "so you are gone. But we will soon find you, no matter how well you have hidden yourself."

'Then he called on his twelve cats to go out all over Erin and search for me, six to go under the ground and six over the ground. He himself sat down under the tree. In a short time the cats, having searched the whole country from top to bottom, came back without finding a trace of me. It was then he chanced to look up into the tree and see me. "Aha," he said, "there you are. I'll soon have you down out of that. Come," he said to the twelve cats, "and gnaw down that tree."

'The twelve cats got around the trunk of the tree then and started to gnaw it across, and it wasn't long before they had it cut through, bringing it crashing down flat on the ground before their leader. But just as it fell I managed to spring on to the branches of the tree next to it. Then they started to gnaw that one down, and at the last moment before it fell, I escaped on to the tree next to that. And so all night they kept on after me, gnawing down each tree I was hiding in, until at last I had reached the very last tree of the forest. Then they started to gnaw that one down, and I did not know what way to escape them now. They had it half gnawed across when who should come along but thirteen terrible wolves, a pack of twelve, and a great fierce wolf who was their leader.

'The wolves charged the cats, and fierce and bloody was the fight between them, until at last the twelve cats and the twelve wolves were all stretched out dead and only the two leaders fought on. Then the leader of the wolves made a fierce snap at the red cat, but the red cat lashed the wolf's head with his tail and made two halves of it. The two of them then fell dead on top of one another. Then I was able to come down out of the tree and go home, but as I climbed down it swayed and creaked under me, for it was cut nearly through.

'Now,' said the Black Thief, 'was I not nearer death that time than this young man?'

'Indeed you were so,' said King Conal, 'and he may go with his life, for I'll not break my word. But I'll have the third one yet, so heat up the oil there, and make it good and hot.'

Then he said, 'Were you ever nearer death than this young man?'

'I was to be sure,' said the Black Thief.

'Tell me about it,' said King Conal, 'and if you were I'll let him go free like his brothers.'

Then the Black Thief told King Conal the third story.

IV

# *The Faithless Apprentice*

'SOME time after practising my trade for a while I had got so clever at it that I took some apprentices to learn it from me,' said the Black Thief. 'Among them there was one young man who was cleverer than all the rest, so I spent most of my time teaching him, for he was quick and eager to learn. After a time I had taught him all I knew and he became a better thief than I was myself.

'About this time there was a giant living in a rocky den at the other end of the country, and as he pillaged and stole from all the great nobles around it was well known that his den was full of gold and riches of all kinds. So I plotted with my apprentice to go one day and get as much of his treasure as we could carry away with us. We set out, and after travelling for many days we reached the giant's den in the mountains. It was an underground cavern in the rocks, and there was only one way into it, and that was down through a deep, dark funnel in the rocks, like a chimney.

'We watched the giant for a few days, and he used to go out every morning and come back in the evening with a bag on his back that we felt sure was full of gold and jewels.

One morning when the giant had left I tied a rope around the waist of my apprentice and began to lower him down through the hole in the rock leading to the giant's den. But when he was half-way down he began to shout and scream at me to draw him up again. I drew him up and then he told me that he was afraid to go down. "Go down yourself," he said, "and I'll take charge of the rope and haul you up again."

'I went down, and when I reached the giant's den I saw great yellow heaps of gold, and shining white heaps of silver and precious stones. I opened the bag and put into it as much as one man could lift, and I sent it up on the rope to my apprentice. Then I called up to him to send down the rope for myself. At first I got no answer but then he shouted down to me:

'"I am finished my apprenticeship now, for I am a better thief than yourself, and you have no more to teach me. Good-bye now, and I hope you'll have a pleasant evening with the giant."

'Then I heard no more from him. I looked around now for some way of climbing out of the giant's den, but there was no way of escaping, for not even a fly could get a foothold on those steep, slippery rocks. After that I saw a heap of dead bodies thrown in one corner of the kitchen. I threw myself down among them, for there was nowhere to hide, and I stretched out pretending I was dead.

'In the evening the giant came back carrying three more bodies. He threw the three bodies on the heap near me, and began to light a fire at the other end of the kitchen, and when it was lighted he hung a great black cauldron of water over it. Then he got a big basket and came down and filled it up with bodies. I was the first he threw in, and he put six others on top of me. He took the basket over to the pot, and turned it upside down on top of it, so that the six bodies fell into the boiling water, but I managed to hang on to the bottom of the basket. Then he laid it face downward in a corner of the kitchen, so I was safe for that time.

'When the giant had eaten his supper he fell fast asleep in the chair. Now I took my chance and crept out from underneath the basket. I went over to the entrance to the den, and there, as luck would have it, I saw the giant's ladder, that he had forgotten to turn around. It was cut out of a tree trunk, and when he had gone up or come down, all he had to do was to turn the steps around and nobody, unless someone as strong as himself, could use it. Up I climbed, and it took me no time at all to reach the top.

'And don't you think I was nearer death that time than this young man here?'

'By my troth you were near enough to it,' said the King. 'So I will pardon him along with his brothers. But it is your own turn now, and maybe it is yourself that I will put into the pot in the heel of the hunt, for I'd say you were never nearer death than you are this minute.'

'Near as I am,' said the Black Thief, 'there was a time when I was nearer.'

'When was that?' asked the King. 'Tell me about it, and maybe I'll let you go free, too, with the others.'

Then the Black Thief told the story of how he escaped from the three giants.

V

# *The Three Giants*

'ONE day,' said the Black Thief, 'I felt tired and hungry, and coming to a house I went in to ask for refreshment. Inside I saw a young woman with a child on her lap. The young woman had a knife in her hand, and she was thrusting it at the child as if she would stab it. The beautiful child was laughing and crowing with delight, but the woman was weeping bitterly.

'"Why are you pointing the knife at the child like that?" I asked her, "and why are you crying so sorrowfully?"

'Then she told me her story:

'"Last year, when I was at a fair with my mother and father, three giants suddenly rushed in among the crowds of people. So surprised was everyone to see them that the man who had a bite in his hand did not raise it to his mouth, and the man who had a bite in his mouth did not swallow it. The giants robbed everyone of all they had, and they snatched me away from my father and mother and brought me here to this place. I was told that I was to marry the eldest giant, but I bound him not to marry me till I was eighteen years of age. I will be that in a few days, and then there will be no escape for me unless someone kills the three giants before then."

'"But why are you trying to stab the young child here?" I asked.

'"Yesterday they brought in this child and told me he was the son of a king. They gave him to me, and asked that I make a pie of him and have it ready for their supper this evening."

'"Do not kill the child," said I. "I have a young pig here that you can put into the pie, and they will not know the difference, for the flesh of a pig is very like the flesh of a child. Let us cut off one joint of the child's little finger to put in the pie, and if they are in any doubt you can show them that."

'So the maiden did as I had bade her, and made the pie with the young pig. The three giants ate the pie with great relish, each saying it was a very good pie but there was not enough of it. The eldest brother then sent the youngest giant down to the cellar to bring up a slice from one of the bodies there, as he was still hungry. The giant came down, and catching a hold of me, cut a large slice off my leg, above my knee. This pleased the eldest brother so much that he came down himself to take me up and broil me before the fire. He caught me up and threw me over his back, but he hadn't gone far when I plunged my knife deep into his heart, and he fell down dead on the floor under me.

'Then the second brother came down to get more to eat also, and he again took me on his back, but I stabbed him, too, and stretched him on the floor, like his brother.

'The youngest brother, who was still waiting at the table for some more to eat, now grew angry, and came down to see what was keeping his two brothers. Seeing them stretched on the floor, he shook them and found they were both dead. He looked around him with surprise, and he noticed me looking at him. He dashed towards me, swinging his great iron club over his head. He aimed for my head and brought the club down with such force that it dug itself into the ground to the depth of a man's knee. But I had stepped aside quickly, and not a hair of my head was hurt. While he was trying to pull his club out of the ground I ran at him, and stabbed him three times in the side. Again he raised the club and aimed a blow at me, but again I stepped aside, and now once more, while he was trying to free his club, I thrust my knife three times into his stomach. But the third time he made for me with his club, a wicked hook of it caught in me and tore a great hole in my side. The giant now fell to the ground and died. But I, too, was weak, and my life's blood was flowing out from my side. But as I was thinking of closing my eyes for ever, the young maiden came running down the cellar steps. When I saw her I got up on my elbow and called out to her:

'" Run as quickly as you can and get the giant's sword, that is hanging on the nail by his bed, and cut off his head."

'She ran off and came quickly back with the sword, and, as brave and as strong as any man, she raised it over her head with her two hands, and cut the head off the giant.

'" Now," said I to her, " I'll die easy."

'" You'll not die at all," said she, " for I'll carry you to the giant's cauldron of cure, and it will heal all your wounds, and you'll be as well as ever."

'And there and then she raised me on her back and hurried off with me to another cellar where the cauldron of cure was kept. She raised me up to the edge to lower me into the cauldron, and as she did so the sight was leaving my eyes, and the death-faint was spreading over my brain. She lowered me into the healing water slowly and gently, and no sooner did that water touch my skin than I was in my health and strength again.

'Wasn't I near death at that second?' asked the Black Thief of King Conal.

'Indeed you were,' said the King, 'and even if you were not, I wouldn't put you into the pot, but I would give you your life, like the others, because only for you I myself wouldn't be here to-day, for I was that child that was to be made into the pie for the giant's supper.' And the King held up his left finger for all to see it was missing a joint.

'My father knew that it was the Black Thief who saved my life,' said the King, 'and he searched the wide world for you to give you a reward, but he never found you. So a hundred thousand welcomes before you, and now I will have a great feast prepared in your honour.'

So the feast went ahead, and when it was all over the King loaded the Black Thief with gold and silver, and rewards of every kind, and he gave the three steeds to the sons of the King of Erin to take back to show to their stepmother.

'When she has ridden around the kingdom with them,' said the King, 'let the horses go, and they will come back to me without fail.'

So the three brothers brought King Conal's steeds back to Erin, and they went to their stepmother, who had been on top of the castle ever since they left, watching for their return.

'You brought back the horses,' said the stepmother.

'We did,' said the brothers, 'but we are not bound to give them to you; your sentence was that we were to go for the horses of King Conal and bring them back here. We have done that.'

And with that they turned the horses around and let them go. Off went the steeds like the wind back to King Conal.

'May I go down into the castle now?' asked the stepmother.

'Not yet,' said the youngest, 'for I did not pass any sentence on you before we left for the game I won from you.'

'And what is your sentence?' asked the angry Queen.

'You are to stay where you are until you find three other sons of a king to go for King Conal's horses.'

When she heard this sentence, she dropped dead from the castle.

II

# THE PALACE IN THE RATH

By *Patrick Kennedy*

EVERYONE from Bunclody to Enniscorthy knows the rath between Tombrick and Munfin. Well, there was a poor, honest, quiet little creature, that lived just at the pass of Glanamoin, between the hill of Coolgarrow and Kilachdiarmid. His back was broken when he was a child, and he earned his bread by making cradles, and bosses, and chairs, and beehives, out of straw and briers. No one in the barony of Bantry or Scarawalsh could equal him at these. Well, he was a sober little fellow enough, but the best of us may be overtaken. He was coming from the fair of Enniscorthy one fine summer evening, up along the beautiful shady road of Munfin; and when he came near the stream that bounds Tombrick, he turned into the fields to make his road short. He was singing merrily enough, but by degrees he got a little stupefied; and when he was passing the dry, grassy ditch that surrounds the rath, he felt an inclination to sit and rest himself.

It is hard to sit awhile, and have your eyes a little glassy, and the things seeming to turn round you, without falling off asleep; and asleep my poor little man of straw was in a few minutes. Things like droves of cattle, or soldiers marching, or big flakes of foam on a flooded river, were pushing on through his brain, and he thought the drums were playing a march, when he woke, and there in the face of the steep bank, that was overgrown with bushes and blackthorn, a passage was open between nice pillars, and inside was a great vaulted room, with arches crossing each other, a hundred lamps hanging from the vault, and thousands of nice little gentlemen and ladies, with green coats and gowns, and red sugar-loaf caps, curled at the tops like old Irish *birredhs*, dancing and singing, and nice little pipers and fiddlers, perched up in a little gallery by themselves, and playing music to help out the singing.

He was a little cowed at first, but as he found no one taking notice of him, he stole in, and sat in a corner, and thought he'd never be tired looking at the fine little people figuring, and cutting capers, and singing. But at last he began to find the singing and music a little tedious. It was nothing but two short bars and four words, and this was the style:

'Yae Luan, yae Morth—
Yae Luan, yae Morth.'
'Monday, Tuesday—
Monday, Tuesday.'

The longer he looked on, the bolder he grew, and last he shouted at the end of the verse:

'Agus Dha Haed-yeen!'
'And Wednesday!'

Oh, such cries of delight as rose up among the merry little gentry! They began the improved song, and shouted it till the vault rang:

'Yae Luan, yae Morth—
Yae Luan, yae Morth—
Yae Luan, yae Morth,
Agus Dha Haed-yeen!'

After a few minutes they all left off the dance, and

gathered round the boss-maker, and thanked him for improving their tune.

'Now,' said the chief, 'if you wish for anything, only say the word, and, if it is in our power, it must be done.'

'I thank you, ladies and gentlemen,' says he, 'and if you would only remove this hump from my back, I'd be the happiest man in the Duffrey.'

'Oh, easy done, easy done!' said they. 'Go on again with the dance, and you come with us.'

So on they went with:

'Monday, Tuesday—
Monday, Tuesday—
Monday, Tuesday,
And Wednesday!'

One fairy, taking their new friend by the heel, shot him in a curve to the very roof, and down he came the other side of the hall. Another gave him a shove, and up he flew back again. He felt as if he had wings; and one time when his back touched the roof he found a sudden delightful change in himself; and just as he touched the ground he lost all memory of everything around him.

Next morning he was awakened by the sun shining on his face from over Slieve Buie, and he had a delightful feel down along his body, instead of the disagreeable *cruith* he was accustomed to. He felt as if he could go from that to the other side of the stream at one step, and he burned little daylight till he reached Glanamoin. He had some trouble to persuade the neighbours of the truth of what had happened; but the wonder held only nine days; and he had like to lose his health along with his hump, for if he only made his appearance in Ballycarney, Castle-Dockrell, Ballindaggin, Kilmeashil or Bunclody, ten people would be inviting him to a share of a tumbler of punch, or a quart of mulled beer.

The news of the wonderful cure was talked of high and low, and even as far as Ballynocrish, in Bantry, where another poor *angashore* of a humpback lived. But he was very unlike the Duffrey man in his disposition: he was as cross as brier, and almost begrudged his right hand to help his left. His poor old aunt and a neighbour of hers set out one day, along with him, along the Bunclody road, passing by Killanne and the old place of the Colcloughs at Duffrey Hall, till they reached Temple-shambo. Then they kept along the hilly by-road till they reached the little man's house near the pass.

So they up and told their business, and he gave them a kind welcome, and explained all the ins and outs of his adventure; and the end was, the four went together in the heel of the evening to the rath, and left the little lord in his glory in the dry, brown grass of the round dyke, where the other met his good fortune. The little *ounkran* never once thanked them for all the trouble they were taking for him. He only whimpered about being left in that lonesome place, and bade them to be sure to be with him at the flight of night, because he did not know what was to take from it.

At last the poor cross creature fell asleep; and after dreaming about falling down from rocks, and being held over the sea by his hump, and then that a lion had him by the same hump and was running away with him, and then that it was put up for a target for soldiers to shoot at, the first volley they gave awoke him, and what was it but the music of the fairies in full career. The melody was the same as it was left them by the hive-maker, and the tune and dancing was twice as good as it was at first. This is the way it went:

'Yae Luan, yae Morth—
Yae Luan, yae Morth—
Yae Luan, yae Morth,
Agus Dha Haed-yeen!'

But the new visitor had neither taste nor discretion; so when they came about the third time to the last line, he croaked out:

'Agus Dha Yaerd-yeen,
Agus Dha Haen-ya.'

It was the same as a cross fiddler that finds nobody going to give him anything, and makes a harsh back-screak of his bow along one of the strings. A thousand voices cried out, 'Who stops our dance? Who stops our dance?' and all gathered round the poor fellow. He could do nothing but stare at them with his poor, cross, frightened face; and they screamed and laughed till he thought it was all over with him.

But it was *not* over with him.

'Bring down that hump,' says the King; and before you could kiss your hand it was clapped on, as fast as the knocker of Newgate, over the other hump.

The music was over now, the lights went out, and the poor creature lay till morning in a nightmare; and there the two women found him, at daybreak, more dead than alive. It was a dismal return they had to Ballynocrish; and the moral of my story is, that you should never drive till you first try the virtue of leading.

# III

# THE THREE SONS OF THE KING OF ANTUA

THERE was a King in Antua at one time, and he had three sons, and they were called Cod, Cead and Michead. One day Cod was walking by the sea-shore when he saw a ship sailing in from the sea. The ship never stopped till it touched land, just near where he was standing. Out of the ship came a beautiful maiden, who walked up the strand to Cod and said to him:

'I put you under bonds to lose your head and all your property unless you will find me and make me your wife before a year and a day.'

'How and where will I find you?' asked Cod.

'One year I am a cat, one year a hound, and one year a white-feathered swan. One day in each of these I am in my own form, and it is not the worst. On that day I am among women. Look for me and find me by your wit and skill.'

Then the beautiful maiden went back to the ship, and sailed away out to sea. Cod then went back to his father's castle, and, throwing himself down on a chair, gave out such a sorrowful sigh that the chair broke under him.

'That's the sigh of a man who has been forced to promise

something that is too difficult for him to perform,' said his father.

'It is the truth you are saying, Father,' said Cod.

'And what promise is it that you made?' asked his father.

'A woman sailed in from the sea to-day, and put me under bonds to find her and to make her my wife within a year and a day,' said Cod.

'Keep up your heart,' said the King. 'I will have a good vessel made ready with provisions for seven years in it. You can take your two brothers with you, and you can search the whole world for the maiden till you find her.'

So the King of Antua had the ship made ready for his sons, and the three of them sailed away from Antua and began their search for the maiden. After sailing on the wide sea for a long time they came to an island. They drew the ship up on the beach, put the tying of a year and a day on it, and went on shore. They walked on into the island until near nightfall when they came to a castle. They knocked at the door. No one answered. They went in. Inside they found no living thing before them but a cat—a small, white cat—and she was sitting on the floor. In the middle of the room they saw a table laid with meat and drink, and every kind of good food. The three brothers sat down and ate a hearty meal.

Then, as night began to draw on, the cat led them to a bed. The three brothers got into the bed and soon fell asleep, Cod sleeping on the outside. As soon as they were asleep, the little cat jumped up and sat on Cod's breast, outside the clothes, and passed the night there purring quietly to herself.

Next morning when the brothers got up their breakfast was ready on the table before them. After breakfast they got ready to leave the castle and go back to their ship, but the cat stood in front of them at the door and motioned them to go back.

'The cat does not wish us to leave,' said Cod. 'Let us stay here for another day and see what happens.'

So they stayed in the castle that day and that night again, and when they made to set out on the following day the cat stopped them at the door again. They decided then to stay a third day and night at the castle. But on the fourth morning, when the cat stood before them to stop them once more, Cod said, 'Let us take no notice of her; we must go this time.'

So they went to their ship and sailed out to sea again. They were not long sailing when a great man on horseback came riding across the sea towards them from the north. The brothers were in great fright to see him draw near.

The big man came up to the ship, twisted the tail of his horse around the mainmast, and began to draw the vessel after him, hither and over across the ocean.

'This man will keep us on the sea till our ship rots under us,' said Cod. 'Go,' said he to Cead, 'and try if you can cut off the horse's tail with your sword. If you can cut one hair, I will cut all the others.'

Cead went to the mainmast, and, drawing his sword, brought it down with all his might on the tail of the horse. The sword slipped down over the tail without cutting one single hair.

'Draw your sword,' said Cod to his youngest brother, 'and see if you can cut even a single hair.'

Michead raised his sword, but just like his brother's, his sword glanced off the horse's tail without cutting a single hair.

Cod himself rose up now and struck his best blow, but his sword cut no hair of the horse's tail, but as little as his brothers'.

'We may give up now,' said he; 'we will never see home or country again.'

So for three days and three nights the horse dragged them over the sea, and then they saw a dark hound leaping towards them over the water.

The three brothers were now in greater dread than ever, for, as Cod said, 'We might have a chance with the horse. But when that hound comes there will be no escape for us at all between the two of them.'

As the hound drew near the ship, the horseman untied the tail of the horse, and rode away as quickly as he could, and the hound, seeing him go, turned around and ran after him. When the horse and the hound were lost to sight the three brothers turned the ship around and made straight for home as quickly as they could go.

When they reached home and told the whole story to the King their father, there and then he had a strong fleet of ships prepared for them, and when the fleet was ready they set sail again.

After they had been sailing for some time, one day they met a fleet that was twice larger than their own.

'Let us raise a battle-flag,' said Cod.

They raised their battle-flag, but instead of another battle-flag, the other fleet raised a peace-flag. So the two fleets drew up alongside one another, and the three brothers met the six young men who were in charge of the larger fleet, and who told them that three of them were the sons of the King of the White Peaks, and three were the sons of the King of the Spotted Peaks. The sons of the three kings grew very friendly, and the two fleets sailed away together. After some time they came to a long headland that was jutting out far into the sea, so far that no land was to be seen on any side beyond it.

'It must be nice sailing along on the other side of that headland,' said the sons of the King of the White Peaks to Cod. 'Send a ship there and we will send two along with it.'

Cod sent one of his ships and the sons of the King of the White Peaks sent two. No ship came back, so the Kings' sons of the larger fleet sent four ships after them, and Cod sent two. So day by day each fleet kept on sending ships after the others, until at last there were only two ships left, one belonging to the six sons of the two Kings, and one belonging to Cod, Cead and Micead. Cod then, thinking it was a trick, and that the ships of the other fleet had attacked and destroyed his, grew angry, and with his two brothers boarded their ship.

'I will kill you all,' he said, 'if any harm has come to my men.'

The six gave no answer, so Cod and his brothers drew their swords and attacked them. After a bloody fight Cod and his brothers got the best of it, and they were just going to kill the leaders of the other fleet, when the whole six of them turned into six balls of fire, and, rising high up in the air, disappeared into the clouds.

Then Cod and his brothers sailed around the point in search of their men. There was no sign of any ship to be seen there, but when they went ashore they found all their men stretched out on the ground dead. Behind the dead men an army was drawn up ready to give battle.

The three brothers then attacked the army, and the fight lasted from dawn till dark, until, at the end of the day, not one was left standing but Cod and his two brothers. Next morning the six sons of the two Kings came and the fight began again. This time Cod and his two brothers killed all the six, but Cead and Michead lost their lives in the fight, and now Cod was all alone.

He put the bodies of his brothers in a box, lined it with sweet herbs, and made up his mind that he would search the world for a magic Healing Water that would bring them back to life.

While Cod was sprinkling the herbs over the bodies of his brothers he saw coming towards him an enormous, hideous hag. Her hair was so long that it swept the ground all around her, and one of her teeth she used as a staff, and one eye served her as a breast-pin. She drew near and began to speak to Cod in a kindly way:

'I heard you were in trouble, so I came to offer you the shelter of my house for the night.'

Cod thanked her, and slept in her house that night, and on the morning he asked her if she had any Healing Water that would bring his brothers back to life.

'I had Healing Water,' said the hag, 'but the Small Giant of the Mountain stole it from me a while ago.'

'Where will I find that giant now?' asked Cod.

'The road that he travelled when he stole the Healing Water is so trodden down that grass will not grow on it for a year and a day,' said the Witch, 'so it will be easy to find the way to his castle.'

So Cod set out without delay for the castle of the Small Giant of the Mountain. When he reached the castle, the door was open but there was nobody inside, but there was a trout broiling in front of the fire. Cod ate the trout, and then he went out again. This time he saw the Small Giant coming home with a fishing-rod over his shoulder. When he saw Cod, the giant began to laugh.

'Why do you laugh, ugly beast?' asked Cod.

'I am laughing with delight at having you for my supper,' said the giant.

'You haven't me yet,' said Cod, and he drew his sword and leaped at the giant.

After fighting for some time, Cod at last managed to tumble the giant, and as he stood over him with his sword the giant cried out: 'Spare my head and I will give you anything you ask.'

'Give me the Healing Water that will bring my brothers back to life,' said Cod.

'I had that Healing Water,' said he, 'but the Big Giant of the Mountain stole it from me.'

'Where will I find the Big Giant of the Mountain?' asked Cod.

'It is easy to find him, for on the road he travelled the day he stole the Healing Water not a spear of grass will grow for seven years.'

Cod then took the head off the Small Giant with his sword, and took the road to the castle of the Big Giant. When Cod reached the castle the giant was not there, but he found a beautiful young woman inside sitting by the fire with a long knife in her hand. Every now and then she would point the knife at her breast, as if she were going to stab herself.

'Why are you pointing the knife at yourself like that?' Cod asked her.

'It is a year and a day since the Big Giant of the Mountain stole me away from my father's castle,' said the maiden. 'I made him promise then not to marry me for a year and a day, and that time will be up this evening. I would rather take my own life than to be here before him when he comes back.'

'Don't give up hope,' said Cod, 'till you see me dead first.'

'Leave here as quickly as you can,' said the maiden, 'for he will surely kill you if he sees you. He has an iron bar with nine knobs on it, and there are nine poisoned hooks sticking out of every knob. If one of the hooks were but to touch your skin, the limb would swell up with the poison and you would die.'

'I am not afraid,' said Cod. 'I am going to fight the giant for the Healing Water to bring my dead brothers back to life.'

The young maiden then made ready some food for Cod, and while he was eating it she kept watch outside, for fear the giant would come and catch him unaware. When Cod had finished, he himself went out to keep watch, and very soon he saw the giant coming, with his fishing-rod over his shoulder. When he saw Cod he put down his rod, and swinging his big iron bar over his head he brought it down with all his strength on the spot where Cod was standing. But Cod had skipped aside, and the bar buried itself in the earth. While the giant was pulling the bar out of the ground Cod thrust his sword three times into the giant's stomach. So the fight went on between them, till at last the giant grew weak from his wounds. Only once did one of the hooks of the giant's bar touch Cod on the calf of his leg, and no sooner it did than the leg began to swell and grow painful at once. But by this time the giant had fallen on the ground and his blood was flowing away out of his body in little streams.

'I will spare your life,' said Cod to the giant, 'if you will give me the Healing Water that you took from the Small Giant.'

'I had that Healing Water till the King of the Forest came and stole it from me,' said the Big Giant.

Cod, hearing this, cut the head off the giant, and lay down to ease the pain of his own wound.

'There is a cauldron of cure in the castle,' said the young maiden, who, seeing the giant dead, and Cod in need of help, came to his aid. 'The cauldron of cure,' she told him, 'will cure all wounds, but will not bring anyone back to life.'

Cod went with her into the castle and bathed his leg in the cauldron of cure and made it as healthy and as strong as ever it was. So pleased was the maiden at seeing the giant killed that she gave Cod a present of a suit of water-clothes. She told him that if he had them on he could walk under the water in the bed of rivers or lakes, or even under the deep sea itself, and that no water could ever drown him. Cod thanked the maiden and set out to find the King of the Forest.

He was walking for a long time when he came to a lake, and as he was passing along the shores of the lake he saw a white pigeon rising up out of the water in the middle of the lake and soaring away up into the sky.

As Cod watched he saw another pigeon rise up out of the lake and fly away up into the clouds like the first one, and so it went on. Every few minutes a pigeon would rise up out of the water and fly away out of sight into the sky.

Cod wondered greatly where the pigeons were coming from, and why they were rising up like that out of the water, and disappearing into the sky. 'I'll soon find out,' he said, and put on his water-suit, and walked down into the lake. He walked on into the water until it closed over his head, and he kept on walking on the bottom of the lake until he came to the deepest part, in the middle, and there he saw a grand castle before him. He walked up to the door and, as there was no one there to stop him, he went inside. He walked up and down the halls and corridors, and he saw nobody or heard nothing till he came to one room where there was a young and beautiful maiden sitting all alone. In one hand she held a staff, and she had a knife in the other, and once every two or three minutes she whittled a slice from the staff, and the slice turned into a pigeon, and the pigeon flew up through the chimney, and rose like a bubble up through the water of the lake. When she saw Cod watching her, she started up in fright.

'Have no fear,' said Cod, 'but tell me who you are, and what you are doing?'

'I am under enchantment, and have been here in this castle for many a day,' said the maiden. 'And this staff which can never be whittled away my father gave me to keep me from thinking and being sad.'

'And how can you be freed from your enchantment?' asked Cod.

'I can never be freed until three stones are taken from three sluices in the Eastern World and thrown into three sluices in the Western World, or until the King of the Forest is killed.'

The maiden then told Cod where he would find the King of the Forest, and Cod left the lake and went on in search of him. When Cod got the first glimpse of the King of the Forest, he drew his sword and started at once to attack him. There were three thousand Small Men, the people of the Forest, gathered around the King, and whenever Cod knocked the head off one of them he sprang up alive again, put his fingers in his mouth to whistle and ran away. So all day long Cod was slaying the Small Men, but as he slew them others ran up and took their places, while those he slew got up and ran away whistling. Then towards the end of the day a dark fog settled down around him and he could scarcely see his hand, but for three days he kept on thrusting with his sword around him, though he could not see at whom he was thrusting. On the third day the young maiden who had been in the castle of the Big Giant of the Mountain came and lifted the fog, and then Cod saw that all this time he had been hitting the corner of the castle wall, thinking he was fighting the King of the Forest himself. Cod now went and attacked the King of the Forest, and in a short time he got the better of him.

'You must be Cod, son of the King of Antua,' said the King of the Forest when Cod had wounded him, 'for the prophets foretold many years ago that you would gain control of the forest.'

'I am Cod, and I want you to give me the Healing Water you took from the Big Giant of the Mountain,' said Cod.

'I had that Healing Water but one day,' said the king, 'when the Cat of Endless Tales took it from me.'

Cod then went off to find the Cat of Endless Tales, but he had not gone far when he saw his two brothers walking towards him with a beautiful maiden between them. Who should she be but the lady who had come to Antua and had put Cod under bonds to find her. She was the Cat of Endless Tales, and she had the Healing Water with her, and that is how Cod's two brothers had been brought back to life.

Cod married one brother to the daughter of the King of the Forest. The youngest brother married the maiden who had been enchanted under the lake, and Cod gave them the lands of the Small Giant of the Mountain and of the Big Giant of the Mountain.

The Cat of Endless Tales was now free from her enchantment, too, for it was the King of the Forest who had put the spell on her, and Cod married her before the year and the day were up.

The whole company then went back to Cod's ship and sailed away and never stopped till they reached the castle of the King of Antua. There is no one who can describe the welcome their father and mother had for the three brothers. The King took the crown off his own head and put it on the head of Cod, and he gave over his whole kingdom and all his power to him from that day.

# IV

# THE HAUGHTY PRINCESS

By *Patrick Kennedy*

THERE was once a very worthy king, whose daughter was the greatest beauty that could be seen far or near, but she was as proud as Lucifer, and no king or prince would she agree to marry. Her father was tired out at last, and invited every king, and prince, and duke, and earl that he knew or didn't know to come to his Court to give her one trial more. They all came, and next day after breakfast they stood in a row in the bawn, and the Princess walked along in front of them to make her choice. One was fat, and says she, 'I won't have you, Beer-barrel!' One was tall and thin, and to him she said, 'I won't have you, Ramrod!' To a white-faced man she said, 'I won't have you, Pale Death!' and to a red-cheeked man she said, 'I won't have you, Cockscomb!' She stopped a little before the last of all, for he was a fine man in face and form. She wanted to find some defect in him, but he had nothing remarkable but a ring of brown curling hair under his chin. She admired him a little, and then carried it off, "I won't have you, Whiskers!'

So all went away, and the King was so vexed, he said to

her, 'Now, to punish your *impedence*, I'll give you to the first beggar-man or singing *sthronshuch* that calls;' and, as sure as the hearth-money, a fellow all over rags, and hair that came to his shoulders, and a bushy red beard all over his face, came next morning, and began to sing before the parlour window.

When the song was over, the hall door was opened, the singer asked in, the priest brought, and the Princess married to Beardy. She roared and she bawled, but her father didn't mind her. 'There,' says he to the bridegroom, 'is five guineas for you. Take your wife out of my sight, and never let me lay eyes on you or her again.'

Off he led her, and dismal enough she was. The only thing that gave her relief were the tones of her husband's voice and his genteel manners. 'Whose wood is this?' said she, as they were going through one. 'It belongs to the King you called Whiskers yesterday.' He gave her the same answer about meadows and cornfields, and at last a fine city. 'Ah, what a fool I was!' said she to herself. 'He was a fine man, and I might have had him for a husband.' At last they were coming up to a poor cabin. 'Why are you bringing me here?' says the poor lady. 'This was my house,' said he, 'and now it's yours.' She began to cry, but she was tired and hungry, and she went in with him.

Ovoch! there was neither a table laid out nor a fire, burning, and she was obliged to help her husband to light it, and boil their dinner, and clean up the place after; and next day he made her put on a stuff gown and a cotton handkerchief. When she had her house readied up, and no business to keep her employed, he brought home *sallies* (willows), peeled them, and showed her how to make baskets. But the hard twigs bruised her delicate fingers, and she began to cry. Well, then he asked her to mend their clothes, but the needle drew blood from her fingers, and she cried again. He couldn't bear to see her tears, so he bought a creel of earthenware, and sent her to the market to sell them. This was the hardest trial of all, but she looked so handsome and sorrowful, and had such a nice air about her, that all her pans, and jugs, and plates, and dishes were gone before noon, and the only mark of her old pride she showed was a slap she gave a buckeen across the face when he axed her to go in an' take share of a quart.

Well, her husband was so glad, he sent her with another creel the next day; but faith! her luck was after deserting her. A drunken huntsman came up riding, and his beast got in among her ware, and made *brishe* of every mother's son of them. She went home cryin', and her husband wasn't at all pleased. 'I see,' said he, 'you're not fit for business. Come along; I'll get you a kitchen-maid's place in the palace. I know the cook.'

So the poor thing was obliged to stifle her pride once more. She was kept very busy, and the footman and the butler would be very impudent about looking for a kiss, but she let a screech out of her the first attempt was made, and the cook gave the fellow such a lambasting with the besom that he made no second offer. She went home to her husband every night, and she carried broken victuals wrapped in papers in her side pockets.

A week after she got service there was a great bustle in the kitchen. The King was going to be married, but no one knew who the bride was to be. Well, in the evening the cook filled the Princess's pockets with cold meat and puddings, and, says she, 'Before you go, let us have a look at the great doings in the big parlour.' So they came near the door to get a peep, and who should come out but the King himself, as handsome as you please, and no other but King Whiskers himself. 'Your handsome helper must pay for her peeping,' said he to the cook, 'and dance a jig with me.' Whether she would or no, he held her hand and brought her into the parlour. The fiddlers struck up, and away went *him* with *her*. But they hadn't danced two steps when the meat and the *puddens* flew out of her pockets. Everyone roared out, and she flew to the door, crying piteously. But she was soon caught by the King, and taken into the back parlour. 'Don't you know me, my darling?'

said he. 'I'm both King Whiskers, your husband the ballad-singer, and the drunken huntsman. Your father knew me well enough when he gave you to me, and all was to drive your pride out of you.' Well, she didn't know

how she was with fright, and shame, and joy. Love was uppermost anyhow, for she laid her head on her húsband's breast and cried like a child. The maids-of-honour soon had her away and dressed her as fine as hands and pins could do it; and there were her mother and father, too; and while the company were wondering what was the end of the handsome girl and the King, he and his Queen, *who* they didn't know in her fine clothes, and the other King and Queen, came in, and such rejoicings and fine doings as there was, none of US will ever see, anyway.

## V

## THE BIRD OF THE GOLDEN LAND

THERE was once a king in Erin and he had three sons. The King was not rich; his lands were few; and the only valuable thing he owned was his crown.

Now, at this time a beautiful bird used to visit the King's castle from time to time, flying in through the windows, and while inside singing the most lovely song that was ever heard from any bird in Erin. Nothing pleased the King more, or made him so happy, as listening to the song of that bird, so he called him 'The Bird of the Golden Land'.

One day each of the King's three sons came to him, one after the other, and said:

'Father, I am of an age to marry; will you find me a wife?'

The King listened to each, but gave no answer. He then began to wonder how he would divide his possessions among them. He knew that his crown was more valuable than his lands, and that the one who got that would have more than the other two together.

'My sons will quarrel over the crown,' he thought sadly.

So, having stayed awake all night trying to solve the riddle, he suddenly hit on a plan. In the morning he sent for his three sons and said to them:

'Nothing makes me so happy as listening to the song of the Bird of the Golden Land. If I had her here in this castle I would live with delight, so whichever one of you brings me the Bird of the Golden Land will get the crown.'

'I will set out at once and find the Bird of the Golden Land,' said the eldest.

'I will search the Eastern and Western World till I find that bird,' said the second son.

'I will go for that bird and bring him home,' said the youngest.

So next morning the three brothers set out and walked all day till nightfall. Then, as they were tired, they went up to a house by the side of the road and asked for a night's lodging. A young woman opened the door to them, and told them they could have a night's lodging and welcome.

'I know,' she said, 'that you are the sons of the King of Erin and that you are seeking the Bird of the Golden Land.'

They went to bed and slept soundly, and next morning, when they had eaten their breakfast, an old man got up from a corner by the fire and said to them:

'I will put you on the right road for what you are searching, and I will go with you and give you all the help and advice I can. Now, let the eldest and strongest take the big sledge-hammer lying outside by the wall, let the second brother of you take the cradle that is beside it, and let the youngest of you take the coil of rope. Now follow me.'

The three brothers took the sledge-hammer, the cradle and the rope, and they set out along the road together, and walked all day till they came to a broad, flat rock.

The old man stopped before the rock and said to the eldest:

'Raise your sledge-hammer now, and strike your strongest blow on that rock.'

The eldest brother did as he was told and struck the rock with a great blow of the hammer, breaking an enormous piece out of it, and making a hole in the middle.

As they looked down through the hole in the rock they

could see a dark opening deep in the ground that seemed to have no bottom.

'Look down now,' said the old man, 'for this is the road you must take if you want to go to the Golden Land. Whichever of you wants to go there must be lowered down in the cradle. If he is lucky he will reach the bottom safely, but he may strike the rocks on the way and be killed. If he is lucky enough to reach the Golden Land, he may win the bird, or he may lose his life.'

'I am not afraid,' said the eldest brother; 'I will go down.'

He got into the cradle and they fastened the rope to it and let him down into the deep, dark hole. But he had not gone very far when the cradle began to strike against the rocks at each side in the darkness, and he shouted at them to draw him up again.

Then the second brother got into the cradle and was lowered down into the dark hole, but very soon he, too, shouted to be drawn up like his brother.

The youngest son said he would try.

'Have you rope enough to carry me to the bottom?' he asked the old man.

'Plenty and to spare,' answered the old man.

So the youngest son got into the cradle and was lowered down and down until at last he reached the bottom. No sooner did the cradle come to rest than the King's son saw a road in front of him. He got out and walked along the road, and very soon he found himself in the most beautiful country. He walked on until nightfall, and then he saw before him a tall, noble-looking castle. He went up to the door and asked for a night's lodging. The young woman who opened the door said:

'A hundred thousand welcomes before you, King of Erin's son.'

The King's son wondered that the young woman should know him, but he was more surprised still when she said:

'I know you and I know what brought you, and I will give you all the help and advice I can. The road to the

Golden Land will take you seven years to travel, and seven more to come back, but if you choose the right horse out of my stables you will be there and back in a day. And remember you must be at the opening to the upper land before a year and a day, for the old man and your two brothers will not wait longer than that to haul you up to Erin once more. Go to my stables now and choose your horse.'

The King's son went to the stables and looked at the horses, but he thought they were all too big and powerful for him. 'If I were thrown by one of these tall horses,' he thought, 'it would kill me.'

So he chose a poor-looking, small mare that he saw behind the stable door. Then he combed and groomed, saddled and bridled her and led her out.

'You have chosen the best horse of all in the stables,' said the young woman when she saw him leading out the mare.

The King's son then mounted, left good health with the young woman, and started out for the Golden Land.

After they had been going along at a great speed for a while the mare spoke and said:

'Look between my ears, king's son, and tell me what you see.'

'I see a broad, rough sea,' said the young man.

'Now,' said the mare, 'if you are the right king's son we will be able to cross over that as if it were dry land.'

After a few minutes they came to the sea and the little mare bounded over the dancing waves as if she were galloping over a meadow. Then they came on to the land again, and they went on for some time over the land and then the mare said to the young man:

'Look between my ears now, and tell me what you see.'

'I see a much broader sea than the one we have crossed.'

'If you are the right king's son we will cross over this one as easily as we crossed the last one,' said the mare.

Then they came to the shore of the second sea, and again the mare rode over the waves as smoothly and easily as if she were on dry land. After another while, after they had crossed the sea, the little mare spoke again and said:

'Look between my ears, king's son, and tell me what you see.'

'A terribly rough, broad sea lies before us now,' said the King's son.

'This is a wild and terrible sea to cross,' said the mare, 'and if you are not the right king's son there will be no escape for us. In this sea there are three small islands, and on them I will rest as we go across.'

The mare plunged off the shore on to the stormy sea and skipped lightly over the high, spitting waves until she came to the first island. There she rested for a while. Then on she rode again till she came to the second island, where she rested again. Then away with her once more till she reached the third island, and then on to the shore. They rode on for many miles then till dusk began to fall, and then they saw a great shining castle before them.

'I wonder who lives in that castle,' said the King's son.

'That is the castle of the King of the Golden Land.' said the mare. 'When we reach it I will ride up to the stables at the back of the castle. There are thirteen stables in it, and as we come to the door of each stable ten stable-boys will run out to take me from you, to groom and stable me. You are to send them away and say you want to attend to your horse yourself. Go on then to the last stable, and there you can dismount and lead me in.'

They rode past the twelve stables, and just as the mare had said ten hostlers rushed out from each one to take the mare from the King's son, but he bade them to stand aside. Then, when he reached the thirteenth stable, he dismounted and led her in. At that moment the King himself came running down the stable yard shouting:

'How dare you take your horse into that stable? Are not my hostlers good enough to look after your mare?'

'I would like to look after my own horse,' said the young man. 'Surely the King of the Golden Land will not deny me the pleasure of looking after my own horse that has brought me safely on such a long journey ?'

'I know well why you have come here,' said the King. 'You are seeking the Bird of the Golden Land.'

'That is the truth,' said the King of Erin's son.

'If you are,' said the King, 'you must win her.'

'I can but try,' said the young man.

'To-morrow at sunrise I will hide and you must find me,' said the King. 'If by sunset you have not succeeded you will lose your head.'

The young man went back to the mare and told her what the King had said.

'What am I to do ?' he said to her. 'The King will hide himself, and if I do not find him I will lose my head.'

'Lie down there under the manger before me, and go to sleep,' said the mare.

The King's son did as the mare bade him, and as he lay in the hay she tipped him with her hoof and he fell fast asleep. Next morning she woke him up with another gentle tip of her hoof.

'Now,' said the young man, 'where shall I find the King ?'

'Go into the garden,' said the mare, 'and take no notice of the King's daughter, or of any of the maidens you will see walking there; even if they speak to you do not answer them. Walk down to the end of the garden, where you will see an apple tree with a single red apple growing on it. Pluck that apple. Cut it in two. The King will be inside in the middle of it.'

The young man went to the garden and saw the beautiful maidens. He passed them all by without as much as glancing at one of them and walked to the end of the garden, where he saw the single red apple growing on the tree. He hurried to pluck it, saying: 'This is the rosiest and most beautiful apple I have ever seen in my life. I will take it back to Erin with me.'

'Indeed you will not take it,' said the King's daughter. 'That apple belongs to my father, and you must not take it.'

'Very well, then, for your sake I will take only half of it.' said the King's son, 'and I will leave you the rest.'

And he drew out his knife, made two halves of the apple, and out jumped the King.

'Oh,' said the King, 'that is one cut on my head to-day.'

'I am sorry,' said the young man, 'but how was I to know that such a mighty king as you would be inside in an apple?'

'To-morrow,' said the King, 'I will hide again, and if you have not found me by sunset I will cut off your head.'

That evening the young man went back to the mare's stable and told her everything. She put him asleep under the manger as before, and in the morning she woke him with a tip of her hoof.

'Go now into the kitchen of the castle,' said she. 'Walk up to the fire. There will be a great many maidens there, but do not take any notice of them. The cook will give you a bowl of broth with no spoon in it. Say "I must find a spoon" and go to the cupboard. There you will see a three-headed pin. Take the pin, cut it open with your knife. You will find the King inside.'

The young man went to the kitchen, and everything happened as the mare told him. He got the broth without a spoon. He went to the cupboard for the spoon and found the three-headed pin, and took it up.

'This is the loveliest pin I have ever seen,' said the young man. 'I will take it home to Erin with me.'

'Indeed you will not take it,' said the King's daughter, 'for it belongs to my father.'

'For your sake I will take only half of it,' said he. 'I will give you the other half.'

And he drew out his knife and cut the pin in two. The King jumped out in front of him.

'Oh,' said he, 'I have two cuts on my head now, one yesterday and one to-day.'

'I am sorry,' said the young man, 'but how was I to know that such a mighty king as you could be in a three-headed pin?'

Then the King told him that he would hide again on the next day, and if he had not found him by sunset he would pay with his head.

The young man went back to the mare again and told him that he had to find the King again on the morrow.

'It will be harder work to find him this time,' said the mare, 'but anyway do as I tell you. Take a few grains of barley with you and go to the pond near the garden. You will see a duck there swimming around by herself. Keep throwing the barley down on the bank till she comes towards you. While she is picking the barley catch her and tell her to lay an egg. She will refuse. Tell her you will kill her unless she lays an egg. She will lay an egg then. The King will be in that egg.'

The next morning the King's son went out to the pond, threw the barley down for the duck, caught her and told her to lay an egg.

'How can I lay an egg when I have none?' said the duck.

'If you don't lay an egg I will kill you,' said the young man.

The duck laid the egg, and the young man took it in his hand and said:

'This is the finest egg I have ever seen. I will take this egg and eat it myself.'

'Indeed you will not take that egg and eat it,' said the King's daughter; 'that egg belongs to my father.'

'I will be generous,' said the young man. 'I will give you half of it.'

With that he split the egg in two. Out sprang the King shouting: 'There are three cuts on my head now.'

'I am sorry, but I never thought that a mighty monarch like you would be hiding in a duck's egg,' said the young man.

'You have beaten me,' said the King, 'for you have found me three times. Now you must hide and I will search for you from sunrise till sunset, and if I find you I will take the head off of you.'

Sadly the King of Erin's son went back to the mare in her

stable and told her what the King had said now. She said nothing, but bade him sleep under the manger as every night. She woke him in the morning with a tip of her hoof.

'Where will I hide from the King?' asked the young man.

The mare turned him into a flea that went hopping around the stable in the hay.

After a while the King came to the stable with a brush and a curry-comb and began to comb and brush the mare and to search the whole stable for the young man, but he could find no trace of the King of Erin's son. He went back to the castle, and the mare gave the young man back his own shape, and said to him:

'Go up to the castle, and when the King will ask you where you were hidden, do not tell him—say that you did not ask him such a question the day he was in the middle of the apple.'

The King's son went to the King in the castle, and everything happened as the mare had said. Then the King said:

'You must hide again to-morrow, and I will look for you. If I find you you will lose your head.'

Next morning the mare roused the young man and turned him into a bee. The King came again and hunted all through the stable, and all around outside it, but not a trace of the King of Erin's son could he find. The King then went back to the castle, and the mare gave the young man back his own shape. Then he sent him to the castle to see the King.

'Where did you hide to-day?' asked the King.

'I did not ask you such a question the day you were hidden in the three-headed pin,' said the young man.

'We'll make another trial to-morrow,' said the King, 'and I may win your head this time.'

Next morning the mare woke the King's son very early and said to him:

'I will turn you into a hair in one of my eyelids to-day.'

Again the King came and searched the stables and all

around it, but not a sign of the young man could he find. At midday he gave up the search and went back to the castle in a very bad temper. The mare put his own form on the King of Erin's son and said to him:

'Go now to the castle. The King will be raging. Answer him not a word, please him in every way. He sleeps only once in seven years. If you please him he will try a night's rest, and all his people will fall asleep with him. You'll find me ready at the door. Grasp the cage that is hanging there, mount me, and away with you.'

The King of Erin's son obeyed all these words carefully. The King went to sleep after his trials and efforts. The young man seized the cage, but as he did it the bird let a scream out of him that roused everyone in the castle. The King's son sprang into the saddle and away he rode.

'Look behind you,' said the mare after a time, when they were in sight of the sea with the three islands, 'and tell me what you see.'

'The largest army I have ever seen is following us.'

'What colour is it?'

'White.'

'We can escape that,' said the mare.

She crossed the sea with the three islands.

'Look again,' said she when in sight of the middle sea.

'A terrible army is after us.'

'What is the colour of it?'

'Red.'

'We may escape that army,' and she crossed the middle sea.

'Look behind,' said the mare the third time when in sight of the third and smallest sea.

'I see a still greater army.'

'What is the colour of it?'

'Black.'

'We can escape that army.'

They came to the smallest sea and crossed over without any trouble, and the army was left on the far side.

At last they reached the castle where the King's son found the mare. The young woman was in front of the castle before him with a hundred thousand welcomes because he had the bird.

'Do you know who that bird is?' she asked.

'I do not,' said the King's son.

'That bird is a Queen with Three Crowns, the mare that carried you is a Queen of Two Crowns, and I am a Queen of One Crown. I have a rod here that will give their right forms to the two Queens. Once she receives her own form again the Queen of Three Crowns will have the power to make a bird of herself whenever she pleases. The Queen of Two Crowns has not that power, and I have no power to change myself, but another might change us with this rod.

'Now, do you know what we'll do? We will give the Queen of Two Crowns to your eldest brother, I will take your second brother, and you will have the Queen of Three Crowns.'

'That is the right thing,' said the King's son, 'if my father is willing.'

'He will be willing,' said the young woman, striking the bird.

The bird became the most beautiful woman that ever the sun shone on. Next she struck the mare, and she was the Queen of Two Crowns.

'It is time for us all to go to Erin. The old man and your brothers will think it too long they are waiting,' said the Queen of One Crown.

All then went to the foot of the opening. The Queen of Two Crowns went into the cradle, and the King's son from Erin shook the rope. The three men above drew up the cradle. The eldest brother took the Queen of Two Crowns for himself. The cradle was let down again and the Queen of One Crown went up. The second brother took her. When the turn came for the Queen of Three Crowns she said:

'Wait a while; put a stone in the place of me.'

The King's son did so, and when the cradle was drawn almost to the top the men above cut the rope, and the cradle fell to the bottom.

The two brothers started for home straight away, each thinking of the young Queen that he was going to marry, but before they reached the house where they took the cradle, the sledge-hammer and the rope, they bethought themselves, remembered their father's promise of the crown, and said to the old man:

'Before we left home we told our father to find wives for us. He did not promise to get us the wives, but he said he would give the crown, which is worth far more than his kingdom, to the man who would bring him the Bird of the Golden Land. We went for that bird, and are going home now without it. What answer are we to give now to our father?'

'I will tell you what to do,' said the old man. 'I saw a rod of enchantment with the second woman. I will use it.' With that he went to the Queen of One Crown, snatched her rod, struck the Queen of Two Crowns, and said: 'Be the Bird of the Golden Land in her cage.' That moment she was a bird in a cage. He gave the rod to the second brother and said:

'Keep that from the woman you are going to marry.'

They went on, came to the old man's house, and spent one night in it. Next morning they started for their father's castle. The old King was glad to see his two sons, but asked in a moment: 'Where is your brother?'

'A rock fell and crushed him on the road,' said the two sons.

'Did you find the bird?'

'I brought her,' said the eldest, and showed the cage to his father.

The King had the cage hung near his window. Though he waited there was no song from the bird.

'That is not the Bird of the Golden Land,' said the King.

'I have that bird,' said the younger brother.

He went to the Queen of One Crown, struck her with the rod, and made a bird of her. Then he brought her to his father, but this bird would not sing any more than the other.

When the two brothers left the opening with the two Queens and the old man, the Queen of Three Crowns made a bird of herself—the Bird of the Golden Land—flew up through the hole, made a strong woman of herself, let down the rope, and drew up the King's son. The two went on after that, and never stopped until they were in sight of the castle; then the Queen of Three Crowns became the Bird of the Golden Land once again, flew to a window of the King's chamber, and began to sing. Inside the window was the cage with the Queen of One Crown in it, in the chamber was the King bewailing his youngest son, and sad because he could not hear the song of the bird.

'O—h,' said the King, springing up, 'that is the Bird of the Golden Land, and my youngest son has her surely.'

The words were scarcely out of his mouth when in came the youngest son with the Queen of Three Crowns, and she told the whole story. The King, in a rage, wished to banish his two wicked sons, but he forgave them in the end.

The second brother took the rod and brought back the other two queens to their own shapes.

The King then settled all his possessions as he wished, and he was happy, for his youngest son was not killed, and he had the Bird of the Golden Land in his castle as he had wanted.

# VI

# THE ENCHANTMENT OF GEAROIDH IARLA

By *Patrick Kennedy*

IN old times in Ireland there was a great man of the Fitzgeralds. The name on him was Gerald, but the Irish, that always had a great liking for the family, called him *Gearoidh Iarla* (Earl Gerald). He had a great castle or rath at *Mullymast* (Mullaghmast); and whenever the English Government were striving to put some wrong on the country, he was always the man that stood up for it. Along with being a great leader in a fight, and very skilful at all weapons he was deep in the *black art*, and could change himself into whatever shape he pleased. His lady knew that he had this power, and often asked him to let her into some of his secrets, but he would never gratify her.

She wanted particularly to see him in some strange shape, but he put her off and off on one pretence or other. But she wouldn't be a woman if she hadn't perseverance; and so at last he let her know that if she took the least fright while he'd be out of his natural form he would never recover it till many generations of men would be under the mould. 'Oh! she wouldn't be a fit wife for Gearoidh Iarla if she could be easily frightened. Let him but gratify her in this whim, and he'd see what a hero she was!' So one beautiful summer evening, as they were sitting in their grand drawing-room, he turned his face away from her and muttered some words, and while you'd wink he was clever and clean out of sight, and a lovely goldfinch was flying about the room.

The lady, as courageous as she thought herself, was a little startled, but she held her own pretty well, especially when he came and perched on her shoulder, and shook his wings, and put his little beak to her lips, and whistled the delightfullest tune you ever heard. Well, he flew in circles round the room, and played *hide and go seek* with his lady, and flew out into the garden, and flew back again, and lay down in her lap as if he was asleep, and jumped up again.

Well, when the thing had lasted long enough to satisfy both, he took one flight more into the open air; but by my word he was soon on his return. He flew right into his lady's bosom, and the next moment a fierce hawk was after him. The wife gave one loud scream, though there was no need, for the wild bird came in like an arrow, and struck against a table with such force that the life was dashed out of him. She turned her eyes from his quivering body to where she saw the goldfinch an instant before, but neither goldfinch nor Earl Gerald did she ever lay eyes on again.

Once every seven years the Earl rides round the Curragh of Kildare on a steed, whose silver shoes were half an inch thick the time he disappeared; and when these shoes are worn as thin as a cat's ear he will be restored to the society of living men, fight a great battle with the English, and reign king of Ireland for two-score years.

Himself and his warriors are now sleeping in a long cavern under the Rath of Mullaghmast. There is a table running along through the middle of the cave. The Earl is sitting at the head, and his troopers down along in complete armour both sides of the table, and their heads resting on it. Their horses, saddled and bridled, are standing behind their masters in their stalls at each side; and when the day comes, the miller's son that's to be born with six fingers on each hand will blow his trumpet, and the horses will stamp and whinny, and the knights awake and mount their steeds, and go forth to battle.

Some night that happens once in every seven years, while the Earl is riding round the Curragh, the entrance may be seen by anyone chancing to pass by. About a hundred years ago a horse-dealer that was late abroad and a little drunk saw the lighted cavern, and went in. The lights, and the stillness, and the sight of the men in armour, cowed him a good deal, and he became sober. His hands began to tremble, and he let a bridle fall on the pavement. The sound of the bit echoed through the long cave, and one of the warriors that was next him lifted his head a little, and said, in a deep, hoarse voice, 'Is it time yet?' He had the wit to say, 'Not yet, but soon will,' and the heavy helmet sank down on the table. The horse-dealer made the best of his way out, and I never heard of any other one having got the same opportunity.

## VII

# FINN MAC COOL, THE GIANTS AND THE SMALL MEN

One day, when Finn Mac Cool and the Fenians lived in Erin, it happened that Finn was taking a walk along by the sea at Fintra when he saw a giant wading in from the sea towards him. As the giant came up the strand he bade Finn 'Good day'. Finn returned the giant's salute, and asked him who he was and what had brought him across the sea to Erin.

'I have come from the Land of the Big Men, and I have a message from our King to Finn Mac Cool.'

'Finn is away hunting at the present time,' said Finn, 'but if you will give me the message I will give it to him as soon as he comes back.'

'The King of the Big Men has heard of the great deeds of Finn Mac Cool,' said the giant, 'and he sent me here to invite him to come to his castle to guard his child that will be born soon, and to keep him safe from the thief who has stolen his other two children. A strong guard of the King's soldiers watched the castle, inside and out, all day and all night, when each of his other two sons were born, but in spite of that someone whipped them off, and no one knows who did it, or where they are to this day.'

'I will give that message to Finn Mac Cool when he comes back,' said Finn.

Hearing this, the giant bade Finn 'Good day', and turned around to go home, walking back into the sea, and Finn watched him go till the water came up over his head.

The next day Finn was strolling along in the same place on the strand when he saw a number of very small men playing hurley on the sands. As Finn went by them he gave them 'Good day'.

'Good day to yourself, Finn Mac Cool, Chief of the Fenians of Erin,' said the Small Men.

'Who are you?' asked Finn, 'and what is your calling?'

'We each have a different trade,' said one of the Small Men.

'Is that so,' said Finn, 'maybe you'd tell me what trade have you yourself?'

'I'm called Lazy Back,' said the Small Man, 'for when I sit down no one in the wide world can stir or lift me, or make me rise again.'

'Sit down there till I see can I take a stir out of you,' said Finn.

Lazy Back sat down and Finn caught a good hold on him around the waist, first with one hand and then with two, trying his best to lift him, but not one inch could he stir the Small Man off of his seat.

'By my word,' said Finn, 'you are speaking the truth, for no man living can lift you.'

Finn then turned to the next Small Man and asked him what his name was, and what he could do.

'My name is Hearing Ear, for I can hear a whisper from the Eastern World as I sit here in Fintra.'

The next of the Small Men told Finn he was called Far Feeler.

'And what do you feel?' asked Finn.

'I can feel an ivy leaf falling in the Eastern World and I sitting here in this place.'

The fourth man told Finn that his name was Knowing

Man, and that he knew all that was going to happen in every part of the world.

The next man said he was known as Taking Easy because he was so clever at stealing.

'What can you steal?' asked Finn.

'Anything I wish,' said Taking Easy. 'I can steal the eggs from under a snipe sitting on her nest, and the snipe is the wariest bird alive.'

The next of the Small Men said his name was Climber, for he could climb the walls of the highest castle in the Eastern or Western Worlds, even if they were made of glass.

'And whatever are you called?' said Finn to the seventh of the Small Men.

'I'm called Bowman.'

'And why is that?' asked Finn.

'Because with my arrow I can hit one midge in a crowd of midges dancing in the air.'

'And what might your name and calling be?' asked Finn of the eighth and last of the Small Men.

'I am called Three Sticks, for I can make anything I choose out of wood.'

'How long would it take you to make a ship for me?' asked Finn.

'While you were turning around on your heel,' said Three Sticks. And to show Finn he was telling the truth he picked up a scrap of wood from among the stones on the beach, and asked Finn to turn around on his heel. Finn did as he was asked, and while his back was turned Three Sticks threw the bit of wood out on the sea, and when Finn turned around again he saw a beautiful ship in front of him on the water.

'Now,' said Finn, when he saw the ship, 'I will sail in her to the Land of the Big Men, and if you will all take service with me and guide me to that land, I will pay you well.'

'We are willing to take service with you,' said the Small Men, 'and we will guide you well, for there is no part of the Eastern World that we do not know.'

So Finn took the eight Small Men into his service, and there and then they went aboard and began to put in stores and food, and to get the ship ready for the voyage to the Land of the Big Men. Then they sailed away, and before many days they reached the Kingdom of the Big Men. Pulling the ship up on the beach, they put the tying of a year and a day on it, and then Finn and the eight Small Men set out for the castle of the King.

The King was so pleased to see the great Finn Mac Cool that he ordered a feast to be prepared in his honour. When the feasting was over he spoke to Finn and told him that a son had been born to him that very day, and that he expected the unknown thief would come that night to steal him.

'My first son was taken away the night after he was born, and the same happened with my second son, so to-night I feel sure the thief will come for the son that was born to-day,' said the King.

'Have no fear,' said Finn; 'I and my men will guard the child for you, and if your son is stolen, in spite of our best efforts, I will answer for it with my head.'

Finn then asked that the strongest chamber in the castle be got ready, and that the child be put into it with two nurses to look after him. Then Finn and his eight Small Men went and sat in the same chamber with the child and his nurses.

After a while Knowing Man spoke to Finn and said:

'You did a foolish thing to put your head in pledge for that child's safety, for to-night he will be stolen in spite of our best efforts.'

'If you know that much,' said Finn, 'maybe you can tell us who is going to steal him.'

'I can indeed,' said Knowing Man, 'for it is the same thief that took his first and his second sons, and that is the King's own sister, who lives in the Eastern World. She is a wrathful witch who quarrelled bitterly with her brother years ago, and now she is stealing away his children out of hatred and spite. By her magic she makes herself invisible, and when she finds the castle guarded and locked before her, she climbs up to the roof and stretches her hand down the chimney, snatches the child out of the cradle and takes it away with her to her castle in the Eastern World.'

When Lazy Back heard Knowing Man tell this he sat down by the hearth, and swore a mighty oath that if the witch put her hand down the chimney that night she would never draw it back up again with the grip he would keep on it.

Then they all sat down to a game of chess to pass the time, but they were not long playing when, a short time after midnight, Hearing Ear called out:

'I hear the witch getting ready to leave her castle in the Eastern World; I hear her telling her servants to guard the King's other two sons well, while she is coming here to steal the third.'

'I feel her going up through the door in the roof of her castle now,' said Far Feeler. 'Her castle has no door, only an opening on the roof, and its high walls are as slippery as glass.'

'Be sure and give us good warning,' said Finn to Hearing Ear, 'when she is drawing near this castle.'

After a short time Hearing Ear said that the witch had arrived, and was walking around outside, and was passing through the sentries without their noticing her, for she was invisible.

'Now is the time for us to be on our guard,' said Finn.

No sooner were the words out of his mouth than the long black hand of the witch came down the chimney, but as soon as it appeared Lazy Back made a grab at it, and he caught such a firm hold of it that nothing the witch could do would free her arm. At last, after a great deal of twisting and pulling, the hag's arm came out of her shoulder socket, and Lazy Back drew it slowly down the chimney and back into the chamber. As he did so, Finn, the two nurses and all the Small Men eagerly gathered around him, to wonder at the length and size of it, and to watch while

Finn measured it with his own, to see which was the longer and the thicker. And so great was their wonder and their curiosity that they forgot the child in the cradle. So, while their backs were turned, the witch stretched down her other hand and drew up the child.

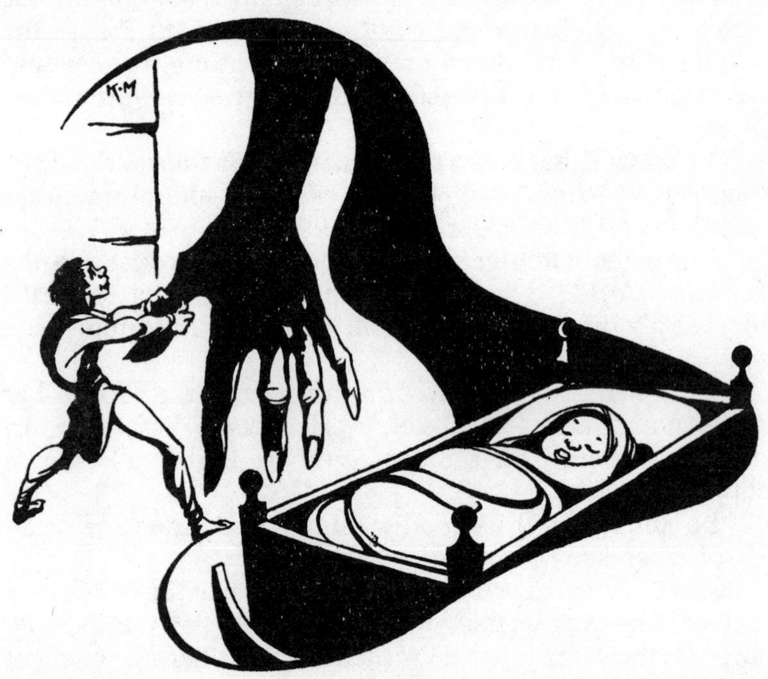

When the two nurses turned around and saw the cradle empty they screamed and they shouted with fright and horror, and the Small Men said:

'Let us go at once back to our ship and sail away, before the King wakes up in the morning, for he will surely take our heads, as well as Finn's, for not keeping a better watch over his son.'

'We will not run away,' said Finn. 'Let us follow the witch and rescue the three sons of the King, and then he will be more pleased than ever.'

So there and then Finn and the eight Small Men set out,

and in a short time they reached their ship and raised sails and went in search of the witch's castle in the Eastern World. After a few days' sailing they reached the Eastern World, and then Climber, Taking Easy and a few others set out for the castle of the witch, leaving Finn, Bowman and some others to guard the ship.

The witch's castle had no door except one high up in the middle of the roof, and its great high walls were so smooth and slippery that a fly would not get a foothold on them. But to scale them was no trouble at all to Climber. So, taking Taking Easy on his back, he went up to the top of the castle as easily and as quickly as if he had wings.

Taking Easy then climbed gently down into the castle, and soon he came back with the youngest of the king's sons. He gave the child to Climber to take down to their comrades, waiting at the foot of the castle walls, and he went down into the castle again. When Climber came up to the top of the castle again, Taking Easy was waiting for him with the second of the King's sons. Climber took this one down, and came up to the top of the castle a third time, and Taking Easy had the third of the King's sons before him. Climber took the third son down to the ground and came back for Taking Easy. Soon they were all on their way back to the ship. When they reached it Finn ordered sails to be raised at once for the Kingdom of the Big Men.

'The witch will follow us,' said Knowing Man, 'and if she overtakes us she will destroy us all.'

'The minute I see her coming towards us I will shoot an arrow at her and kill her on the spot,' said Bowman.

'She is making ready to come after us now,' said Hearing Ear. 'She has found out that the three sons of her brother have been taken, and she is raging around her castle. She has left now, and is racing after us.'

'Far Feeler,' said Finn, 'be ready to tell us when she is drawing near.'

'She is coming after us with great speed,' said Far Feeler. 'She is coming very near us now.'

Bowman got ready, and the instant he caught sight of the

witch he loosed an arrow at her that flew straight at her head and pierced her one eye in the middle of her forehead. No sooner did the arrow touch her than the witch crumbled up and fell dead into the sea.

Finn and the Small Men sailed on quickly now for the Land of the Big Men, and when they reached it they made straight for the castle, where they arrived just one hour before daybreak. Then they took the King's three sons into the strong chamber where the child's two nurses were still waiting, and they put the young child back into the cradle. Then they sat down and rejoiced and made merry while they waited for the King to wake.

Just as the dawn was breaking the King sent a messenger to see how it had fared with his young son during the night. The messenger went to the strong chamber and put his eye to the keyhole, and there he saw the fun and merriment going on inside; he went back and told the King what he had seen.

'They are singing and gaming and telling stories within, and there are two young fellows there that are bigger than Finn Mac Cool himself.'

When the King heard this he knew that his child was safe, for it is certain they could not be making merry if he had been stolen. So throwing on his mantle he went himself to the strong chamber and knocked on the door.

Finn himself opened the door for the King, and showed him the child in the cradle and his other two long-lost sons. Great indeed was his delight at seeing them again and having all his three sons together under his roof once more. He warmly thanked Finn and the Small Men, he had a great feast prepared in their honour, and he loaded them with jewels and riches and every kind of reward. The feast lasted seven days and seven nights, and all the time the eating and drinking and merriment were going on, the King's men were going backwards and forwards between the castle and Finn's ship loading it with jewels and riches of every kind as a reward for saving the three sons of the King of the Big Men from the Hag of the Eastern World.

K·M

# Glossary

*Angashore* a pitiable wretch.

*Bawn* the pleasure grounds of a castle or noble dwelling.

*Birredh* a cap.

*Bothy* a rude shelter or hut in the woods.

*Brishe* fragments. 'To make brishe of' a thing means to break it into smithereens.

*Cantred* a division of land, a district which had to yield one hundred men to fight for the owner in times of war.

*Cruith* form or shape.

*Currac* a boat made of hides, still used in the West of Ireland.

*Curragh of Kildare* the great plain of Kildare, famous for horse-racing since very early times.

*Dun* a fortified dwelling.

*Eric* a penalty, usually a fine, imposed by a dead man's family on the one who has caused the death.

*Keeve* a vat for holding liquid in brewing.

*Ogham* ancient Irish alphabet; generally used on stone monuments.

*Ounkran* a cranky, diminutive creature.

*Rath* a circular dwelling within a fort.

*Reek* a large pile of turf built up in the shape of a haystack.

*Samain time* November in modern times. In ancient days it was the time of an old pagan festival.

*Sheiling* a bower or shelter in the woods, made of interwoven branches.

*Sthronshuch* a stranger.

*Torc* a neck ornament of thin strands of gold twisted in the form of a chain.